Public Sector Reform in Developing Countries
A Handbook of Commonwealth Experiences

Published by:

Commonwealth Secretariat
Marlborough House
Pall Mall
London SW1Y 5HX
United Kingdom

Designed by kcgan designs

Copyright © Commonwealth Secretariat 2001

May be purchased from:

Publications Unit
Commonwealth Secretariat

Telephone: +44 (0)20 7747 6342
Fascimile: +44 (0)20 7839 9081

ISBN: 0-85092-711-0

Price: £12.00

Printed by Abacus Direct

Public Sector Reform in Developing Countries

A Handbook of Commonwealth Experiences

Managing the Public Service
Strategies for Improvement Series: No.14

Edited by Victor Ayeni

Commonwealth Secretariat
2002

CONTENTS

FOREWORD

In early 2002, the Governance and Institutional Development Division (GIDD) of the Commonwealth Secretariat was formed by the merger of Management and Training Services Division (MTSD) and General Technical Assistance Services Division (GTASD), and operates as part of the Commonwealth Fund for Technical Co-operation (CFTC). Its purpose is to strengthen good governance in member countries through providing advice, training and expertise to build capacity in institutions throughout the Commonwealth. It has in-house specialist expertise in governance, including public sector reform and restructuring, public-private sector partnerships, and public sector informatics, but is also able to provide assistance across a wide range of development issues to meet the particular needs of individual member countries.

This publication, which is a continuation of the Commonwealth Secretariat's *Managing the Public Service: Strategies for Improvement series*, is the first under the new division. Through the series, the Commonwealth Secretariat seeks to provide the reader with access to the experiences and successes of institutions and officials from across the Commonwealth. A strong and achieving public service is a necessary condition for a competitively successful nation. However, as the range of structural options and accountability relationships utilised within the public sector increases, the complexity and diversity of that sector is growing. Assessing the strategic options for the public sector requires a clear understanding of the managerial alternatives and the actual and potential capacities of the public service.

The current title, *Public Sector Reform in Developing Countries: A Handbook of Commonwealth Experiences*, is a significant contribution towards that understanding. The publication provides a country-by-country synopsis of the reform experience of about 40 Commonwealth developing states, spread across Africa, Asia, the Caribbean, Europe and the Pacific. It presents a brief profile of each country and the background to the recent political and economic changes. This is followed by an outline of the key reform initiatives, the implementation processes, the achievements, and problems encountered. Wherever possible, each section concludes with a sketch of proposed initiatives and future programmes.

The publication aims to facilitate the sharing of experiences and good practices through a comprehensive but easily accessible focus on the experiences, successes and achievements of developing Commonwealth countries.. In this regard, it provides a seminal departure from the existing literature in the area of public sector reform, which largely concentrates on the individual experience of the developed countries. *Public Sector Reform in Developing Countries* offers a wealth of background information for policy makers, practitioners and trainers. It will no doubt enrich the continuing reform efforts in not only the Commonwealth but also other developing and, indeed, developed countries.

Public Sector Reform in Developing Countries represents a uniquely important addition to our portfolio of publications concerning the management of the public service inherited from the former MTSD. In addition to exposing the immense achievements of Commonwealth developing countries in public sector reform, it is my firm belief that this new title will further contribute to providing the firm ground on which policy makers and officials who are faced with the challenge of public service reform can stand while assessing the options available for the future.

Ms Tendai R W Bare

Director
Governance and Institutional Development Division
Commonwealth Secretariat, London

ACKNOWLEDGEMENT

The materials for this publication have been drawn mostly from background papers and presentations prepared by participants and facilitators of the series of top-level seminars the Commonwealth Secretariat has run in Singapore and New Zealand over the last decade or so. We are grateful to these authors (listed in the Appendix), and to all those who have worked with us on these programmes over the years.

In particular, our gratitude goes to the Singapore Civil Service College and the Graduate School of Management of the Victoria University of Wellington who have organised and played host to the various activities. Similarly, in addition to funding provided under the Commonwealth Fund for Technical Co-operation, the Singapore Development Co-operation Programme and the New Zealand Ministry of Foreign Affairs and Trade have consistently provided significant additional sponsorships for the seminars.

The huge assistance of Ms Alice Cheung, Mr William Rezel and Ms Ayo Davies, colleagues at the Commonwealth Secretariat, both towards the organisation of the seminars and in the preparation of the manuscript is most appreciated. Equally, thanks are due to Ms Maureen Ofili-Njaka for her editorial assistance, and to KC Gan who did the final typesetting. As usual, the dedication and support of Mr Rupert Jones-Parry, the Commonwealth Secretariat's Publications Manager, contributed greatly to seeing this work to fruition. We thank him too.

Victor O Ayeni

Deputy Director
Commonwealth Secretariat, London

INTRODUCTION

Over the past two decades, reforming public sector institutions has been a central concern in developed as well developing countries around the world. Reforming organisations is probably as old as public administration itself, however the current agenda reveals a number of distinguishing features. Not only is it a largely global movement, its message also has been sustained and largely unambiguous. In fact it is for these reasons that some observers have described this reform movement as a 'global revolution'. Clearly, there is a strong political salience to this. Many have talked about a preoccupation with 'hallowing out the state', and a fundamental re-thinking of the role of the state and government, and covering the institutions and processes by which they operate. Equally, the current reform regime has been closely associated with economic and political developments around the global in recent decades, including the demise of the former Soviet Union and subsequent decline of the communist ideology. Lastly, and particularly in the case of developing countries, international creditors and donor institutions have greatly contributed to the pressure on countries to fall in line with the popular changes.

Countries around the world have implemented various public sector reform programmes, mostly patterned around so-called 'new' Public Management (NPM) ideas. The goal is the transfer of private sector management practices, introduction of market forces to government, and establishment of liberal democratic principles. As Ian Scott aptly observed in his contribution to *Public Sector Reform* (co-edited by Ian Thynne), "Government is now seen as public business, profitable where possible, explicitly cost-conscious where not. Civil servants have been transformed into managers. Citizens have become customers or clients with – at least in theory – consumer rights." Obviously, these programmes have not been about transforming public administrative institutions alone. Often they have been accompanied by other political, economic and even social reforms, which have in the main compounded the various implementation processes.

There are significant variations in the details of the different reform experiences. This point is evident later in this book. In the meantime, an important implication of this is that older, more familiar concepts such as 'Administrative reform' or 'Administrative change' are inadequate characterisation of the recent developments. What is more, some observers find such terms too closely associated with the failures of past reforms and the disappointment that is the very focus of the recent change efforts. On the other hand, concepts such as 'Civil service reform', 'Public enterprise reform', 'Health sector reform', 'Local Government reform', etc can be seen as mere sub-elements of the recent movement. Increasingly, there is a strong preference for 'Public sector reform', which many scholars would argue embraces these various strands and sub-elements. In this publication, the concepts of 'Public sector reform' and 'Public Management reform' are used interchangeably and in an encompassing sense to cover the range of structural changes governments around the world have recently implemented to improve the administration of their public sector (see Box I).

The concept 'Reform' conjures several different meanings. Mark Turner and David Hulme have rightly suggested in their book, *Governance, Administration and Development*, that these different meanings ultimately convey a number of common elements. There are about seven of these, namely:

- Deliberate planned change

- Innovation and Improvement

- Need to cope with uncertainties and rapid change, which in turn calls for some urgency

- Heavy technical content but also an inherently political process

- Target at specific institutional issues or system-wide change

- Means to an end, not the end itself

- Involving a combination of strategies and approaches

Overwhelmingly, recent public sector reform programmes have been introduced against a backdrop of widespread disappointing failures in public administration and the state institution at large. Implementing reforms became the means to reinvigorate the state and bring about improvements in the use of resources and, ultimately, better quality of life for society. No country, rich or poor, developed or developing could claim that it was not affected, and so needed to introduce some reform. Soon, reforming also became a 'must-have' ticket for acquiring international respect and credibility. This reform mood remains pervasive and is sure to be so for decades to come. There are good reasons for this conclusion. First, the international environment is changing constantly and bringing up new demands and challenges. Next, there is what may be called important unfinished business, serious matters that are still to be brought to fruition, even in countries that have made phenomenal progress recently. Equally important, is the need to consolidate the few gains that have been made in many countries. In any event, the constant need for improvement and fine-tuning will ensure that the current reform agenda is kept alive for as long as market principles and liberal democratic values continue to hold universal ideological sway. Lastly, there are the continuing pockets of resistance to serious change in many countries. Paradoxically, unless these grow soon into a more dominant force, they are likely to remain ready ammunition for those seeking to justify the need for radical change.

In this circumstance, the Commonwealth has emerged as a veritable force for change. Thus, in 1995, Commonwealth Heads of Governments (CHOGM) endorsed the 'Commonwealth Initiative for Public Service Reform' to provide a focus of collaboration between member governments as they face the challenge to improve public service performance. Called 'Towards a new public administration', the initiative itself was part of a broader Commonwealth effort to fulfil more effectively its commitment to the promotion of good governance as enunciated in the 1991 Harare Commonwealth Declaration. The Commonwealth public administration initiative is founded on a realisation that the public service in all countries is under pressure as never before. It is faced with new tasks, yet staffed with people skilled to achieve old ones. At the same time, the public service faces ever-growing pressures from taxpayers, from politicians compelled to address mounting government debt, and from international donors demanding cuts in government budgets. Parallel to these, citizens have become more active and vocal consumers, and are able to insist on lower costs accompanied by higher quality. Evidently, the public service needs serious improvement to enable it rise up to the prevailing challenges. It must be equipped with the necessary resources, infrastructure, services and regulatory architecture necessary for national competitive success.

Commonwealth countries have, indeed, become widely respected for the success of their reform efforts to bring about this new-style public service. The experience of Commonwealth countries such as Australia, Canada, New Zealand and the United Kingdom that are members of the Organisation for Economic Co-operation and Development (OECD), is nowadays commonly presented as a model for the rest of the world. Equally, other non-OECD Commonwealth member countries such as Malta, Malaysia, Mauritius, Singapore and South Africa, among others, have recorded remarkable economic and political achievements in recent years. However, although a good deal has been written and documented about the experiences of the four Commonwealth OECD members, the contributions of developing countries have been sparsely recorded. This adds up to some 50 countries, about half of which are small and island states. At best, information about these experiences may be found in technical reports prepared by international lenders and donor agencies. But these are hardly readily available or even shared amongst international agencies themselves. A number of problems have resulted from this situation.

First, is the tendency is to take for granted or simply assume that most developing countries are not reforming their public organisations. Clearly this is unhelpful for countries that may be already in desperate situations and badly need to prove that they are at the cutting-edge of an increasingly competitive world. Further, it is difficult in the absence of evidence of their concrete experiences to adequately guide these countries in their improvement efforts. Driven by a widely held belief that public management concerns are generic, the convenient thing to do is usually to copy from the famous programmes without sufficient regard to environmental differences. This is the 'quick-fix' approach. But successful reforms thrive on adequate information about what works well in particular circumstances. This lack of information does not help the self-confidence of developing countries either. Our experience in the Commonwealth Secretariat of working with developing countries reveals a striking tendency in these countries to overly depend on foreign advisers, and to ignore whatever has been done or achieved. The consequence is that reform programmes tends to be caught in an endless cycle of uncompleted ideas that stops and begins with every new adviser that comes to town.

This publication is set against the backdrop of these serious shortcomings. The overriding objective is to focus the developments in Commonwealth developing countries, and make that information more widely accessible. The book aims to facilitate the sharing of experiences and good practices through a comprehensive but easily accessible focus on the experiences, successes and achievements of the countries. In this regard, it offers a seminal departure from the existing literature in the area of public sector reform, which as already pointed out, largely concentrates on the individual experience of the developed countries. The publication offers a wealth of background information for policy makers, practitioners and trainers. The reader is able to know at a glance what reforms have been implemented, and from which experiences additional information may be acquired. Similarly, ready comparison can be made between countries of similar attributes, leading to conclusions on the range of options that are open to them based on lessons of experience. The priority is to complement the continuing reform efforts in not only the Commonwealth but also other developing and, indeed, developed countries.

The book is designed as a quick reference, resource material on public sector reform in Commonwealth developing countries. It presents a country-by-country synopsis of the reform experiences of 40 states, including: 17 African states; 7 in Asia; 7 independent and 2 dependent Caribbean states; 2 in Europe; and 3 independent and 2 dependent Pacific states. Together, these make up about two-third of the membership of the Commonwealth. Remarkably, too, about sixty per cent of the countries covered are small states, providing a fine juxtaposition of the 'big' and the 'small' that makes the Commonwealth a unique body. Evidently, the concept of 'developing countries' is used very loosely here as the countries covered vary markedly from the high income technologically advanced Asian countries to the least developed heavily indebted countries in Africa.

Each contribution starts off with a brief profile of the country covered and the background to the recent political and economic changes. This is followed by an outline of the key reform initiatives, the implementation processes, the achievements, and problems encountered. Wherever possible, each section concludes with a sketch of proposed initiatives and future programmes. The individual country-profile is based largely on the in-puts of officials from the countries concerned, people who have been closely involved in design as well as implementation but whose perspectives are, ironically, usually taken for granted in published works. The materials provide a bridge between theory and practice, drawing attention to what is actually happening on the ground and to often less obvious experiences. Each contribution presents the situation as it is, and avoids making any judgement as such. Obviously, this has its drawbacks; for example the fact that the materials appear lacking in serious analyses, and sometimes only manage to cover a limited aspects of the programme being implemented. This is one price that we were forced to pay to keep the book to a reasonable size. However, it also goes to show that this is invariably a continuous effort that requires, like the reform it seeks to portray, continuous improvement and fine-tuning. Useful suggestions from readers in this regard are welcomed.

All told, several conclusions can be drawn from the information presented in this material about the contemporary reform experience in Commonwealth developing countries. These include:

◆ The current reform movement is a worldwide phenomenon that has touched Commonwealth countries profoundly as well. But the challenge for these countries remains huge and very serious

◆ There is hardly any Commonwealth country that has not embarked on one form of partial or system-wide reform programme. The materials in this book clearly debunk the myth that little or nothing has actually been happening on the reform front in Commonwealth developing countries

◆ Commonwealth developing countries have continued to rely heavily on the received agenda fashioned largely by their OECD counterparts and imported by international creditors and donor institutions

◆ At the same time, there is a clear need to focus more serious attention on the implementation of programmes already adopted, and the development and use of indigenous capacity

◆ Notwithstanding common Commonwealth public administration traditions, there are identifiable differences based on history, culture and geo-political realities that have managed to find their way to the prevailing reform programmes. Similarly, there are noticeable differences in terms of content and emphasis even on similar issues

◆ The outcome of reform has been mixed at best: limited and often scattered successes; many outright failures; several pockets of uncertainties; and persistent economic and governance crises. The best success stories remain those countries that had made appreciable strides in any case before the current swell of reforms

♦ Ownership remains a very serious issue, and this is compounded by a hidden suspicious in many countries that the current reform wave may yet proved to have been over-sold

♦ It is not always evident that countries understand that reform is the means to an end, and not the end in itself. What is more, there is as yet no guarantee that any particular combination and sequence of reform issues will achieve the desired ends

♦ There is an embarrassing lack of serious attention to the linkage between reform of the public service and several of the serious governance crises that the countries face, such as the problem of widespread poverty, social inequalities, the HIV/AIDS pandemic, the persistence of military conflicts, etc. By the same token, this also raises the critical need to make this reform experience more relevant to the achievement of the United Nations development goals published recently.

Box 1: What is Public Management Reform?

Public management reform consists of deliberate changes to the structures and processes of public sector organizations with the objective of getting them (in some sense) to run better. Structured change may include merging or splitting public sector organizations (creating a smaller number of departments to sharpen focus and encourage specialization). Process change may include the redesign of the systems by which applications for licenses or grants or passports are handled, the setting of quality standards for health care or educational services to citizens or the introduction of new budgeting procedures which encourage public servants to be more cost conscious and/or to monitor more closely the results their expenditure generate. Management reform frequently also embraces changes to the systems by which public servants themselves are recruited, trained, appraised, promoted, disciplined and declared redundant.....Here public management consists, in effect, of a benign merger between generic (overwhelmingly commercial, private sector) management and the more traditional concerns of public administration. The concern for democratic values is fully retained but the enterprise is given a sharper cutting edge in terms of risk-taking, flexibility, performance measurement and goal achievements...... 'Reform' is only one among a congeries of alternative and competitive terms (including, significantly several from business world, such as 'transformation' and 'reinvention', as well as others with a longer public sector history, such as 'modernisation' and 'improvement'). Like all these other words 'reform' is a 'loaded' term, in the sense that it strongly implies not just change but beneficial change – a deliberate move from a less desirable (past) state to a more desirable (future) state.....(However) the outcomes of many management reforms have very much depended upon the nature of the administrative-political systems in which they have taken place.

Source: C. Politt and G. Bouckaert, Public Management Reform: A Comparative Analysis, Oxford, Oxford University Press, 2000, pp 6-17

AFRICA

Botswana

Country Profile

Location: The Republic of Botswana is situated in Southern Africa and is bordered by South Africa, Namibia, Zambia and Zimbabwe.

Capital: Gaborone

Area: 582,000 sq km

Population: 1,518,000 (1997). About 90 per cent are of Setswana-speaking origin and most of the rest of Kalanga-speaking origin. Most of Botswana's main settlements are in the south-east of the country.

Language: Setswana is the national language; English is an official language.

Government: Botswana adopted its name on independence in 1966. The country is a parliamentary democracy with an Executive President chosen by the National Assembly for the concurrent year. The House of Chiefs advises on tribal matters.

Economy: Classified as an upper middle-income country, Botswana has come a long way since independence in 1966 when it was ranked among the world's poorest nations. The country inherited little in the way of economic or social infrastructure. Agriculture was the mainstay of the economy. However over the past decades, Botswana's economic performance has been remarkable and has contrasted sharply with the problems experienced by most of sub-Saharan Africa. Botswana has benefited from a stable social structure (it has an unbroken record of parliamentary democracy) and a wealth of natural mineral resources.

But the country faces a crucial test as attempts are made to develop the economy away from a rapid diamond-led growth (Botswana is the largest exporter of gemstone diamonds) to a more diversified and sustainable economic structure. Furthermore, recent difficulties including international recession, a depressed world diamond market, crippling drought in the country, high inflation, an alarming growth in unemployment, the spread of HIV/AIDS and poverty all pose new challenges to Botswana.

Quality and Productivity Concerns in the Public Sector

Botswana has always taken the initiative to introduce necessary changes in its public service to keep it abreast of changing time. More recently, the government has undertaken a number of reforms in the public sector as a way of raising productivity. The problems facing the country are the continuing dominance of the economy by the mining sector, lack of technology to produce high quality products that can compete in global markets, high unemployment rate due to low growth in other sectors of the economy and inadequate skilled labour force, which also contributes to low growth in other sectors of the economy. The public service has been unable to retain the services of qualified staff. Many government projects overrun their budgets, some others are completed late while yet others do not meet the need of customers, thereby resulting in white elephants and nugatory expenditure. Corruption is increasingly a serious problem, with many organisations seemingly uninterested in adhering to the code of ethics. Public complaint against civil servants also includes low level of satisfactory provision of service without a smile.

Public Sector Reform Issues

Highlights of reforms undertaken in the last decade in the public sector include:

◆ an effective human resources management system which places emphasis on trained manpower; personnel performance appraisal system; an appropriate incentive and reward scheme aimed at attracting and retaining skilled personnel, particularly those with scarce skills. This last is being achieved through the implementation of the grand loan scheme for the tertiary education enhanced entry grades for graduates and parallel progression for scarce and skilled manpower;

◆ decentralisation of personnel functions to line ministries. The aim is to enable ministries and departments directly manage and focus on the training and administration of their human resources;

◆ the setting up of the Botswana National Productivity Centre whose mandate is to raise productivity in both the public and private sectors of the economy;

◆ commercialisation and privatisation of certain activities of government which are best done by the private sector;

◆ introduction of Work Improvement Teams Strategy (WITS) in the public service;

◆ introduction of the Performance Management System;

◆ implementation of a Computerised Personnel Information System (the pilot phase for this project was successful);

◆ bench-marking;

◆ Business Process Engineering;

◆ review of public service regulations and policies to make them responsive to the emerging challenges of the twenty-first century;

◆ Organisation and Methods reviews of line ministries and departments to define their objectives and functions in an effort to make them more efficient;

- establishment of the Office of the Ombudsman in an effort to bring more transparency into the operations of government;

- Service Plus Training – teaching skills necessary for good customer service to all levels of staff. (The Botswana Development Corporation has come up with standards which can be used to measure performance of its staff so that the country can be at the same level with leading global players);

- standards – six broad areas have been identified, namely, a full day's work, punctuality, customer calls, response time, effective communication and house keeping.

CAMEROON

Country Profile

Location: Cameroon is situated in West Africa and is bounded by the Gulf of Guinea, Nigeria, Chad, Central African Republic, Congo, Gabon and Equatorial Guinea. The country's geographical location provides transit facilities for the Economic and Monetary Community of Central Africa (CEMAC) member states, namely Central African Republic, the Republic of Congo, Equatorial Guinea and Chad.

Capital: Yaounde

Area: 475,442 sq km

Population: Cameroon has a population of over 14 million from more than 200 ethnic groups. About 45 percent of the population live in the urban areas.

Language: French and English are both official languages.

Government: Cameroon which gained full independence in 1960 is often likened to the political laboratory of Africa, having experienced during its colonial history the different systems of government from German, French and British colonial rule. The country is a unitary republic with a multiparty presidential democracy.

Economy: Thanks largely to its oil wealth and agricultural diversity, the economy of Cameroon went through a long period of prosperity until the economic crisis in the 1985/86 fiscal year. The social and economic consequences of this crisis are evidenced by a pronounced decrease in the state's resources as well as in the resources of the private, agricultural and domestic sectors; reduction in government salaries; marked increase of workers laid off and the degradation of basic social services and essential infrastructure.

Quality and Productivity Concerns in the Public Sector

The people that the public sector in Cameroon has to serve are heterogeneous in many ways. Ethnic nationalism plays a significant role as each group struggles for a share of the national cake. Superimposed over this ethnic diversity are the two colonial legacies of English and French which have shaped the present administrative structure in Cameroon. Some of the major concerns of the public about the public sector are as follows:

- the public feel that they are too far removed from the decision making process and that local realities are not usually considered (the centres where services are provided are usually located in the capital or provincial headquarters, far away from the majority of the people);

- the public feel that they are perceived as intruders in those places where services should be rendered to them;

- on many occasions, officers responsible for a given service are not available when needed by the public;

- communication between the state employee and the public is sometimes hindered by language and attitude barriers.

On the other hand, the following may be considered as difficulties encountered by state employees in carrying out their role of providing service:

- lack of proper professional knowledge and as a result, only a partial understanding of the needs of the public;

- poor distribution of staff and lack of appropriate equipment and infra-structure to adequately produce and deliver services (for example, there may be too many workers in some offices with some not having work tables while there may be too few staff in some other offices);

- low salaries.

Another important factor that affects service delivery in the public sector is the attitude of employees, especially those at the lower and middle cadres. Many of them are in no hurry to complete an assignment so as to proceed to the next one. The popular belief is expressed in the following statement that has been repeated over the years: 'Administration never runs out; we met it and we shall leave it behind.'

Public Sector Reform Issues

Over the years, changes in the public sector have shifted considerably from simply making new rules to carrying out administrative action in a more efficient manner, and limiting administrative activities to only some domains. These changes have included:

- introduction of a new set of rules contained in a decree published in 1994, establishing the General Rules and Regulations of the Public Service;

- a National Programme for Good Governance;

- a programme of privatisation;

- reorganisation of ministries;

- the fight against corruption and poverty.

The 1994 General Rules and Regulations of the Public Service states that any job position must first be provided for in the state budget and shall correspond to tasks, duties and responsibilities requiring special skills and aptitudes. It further states that a competent authority shall appoint persons to different job positions. The National Programme for Good Governance is expected to usher in further positive changes in the public sector. There is a relentless campaign against corruption, which has been responsible for inefficiency and laxity in the administration.

One area in which change has been most significant is in the recruitment and training of state personnel. At independence, the void left by the departure of foreign civil servants had to be filled locally and quality of personnel was not a priority at the time. Furthermore, the issue of ethnic nationalism and the distribution of the national cake played a great role in the recruitment process. Annually, persons were recruited into the civil service with no specific duties defined. For example, in the late 1980s, the President ordered the mass recruitment of 1,500 unemployed young people into the public service. While this apparently solved a political problem, it created another for the Ministry of the Public Service that had to locate appropriate jobs for these recruits. Fortunately, given the changing environment of the public sector, such recruitment is no longer possible.

A number of professional schools were created at independence to select and train future civil servants. Once in any of these schools, a candidate was assured of becoming a civil servant on completion of the course. A lot has since changed on this front. For example, the numbers selected for training are strictly matched with the needs in each field, which are constantly being updated.

In the continuous strive for improvement, the Cameroon public sector has gone through many stages. There is now a shift from a civil service in terms of career to a civil service in terms of duty post. The former provided jobs for those recruited from point of entry and they progressed periodically to the end of their career. No specific results were expected from these employees. However, achieving results has become a requirement from state employees who are now recruited on the basis of available posts and who must be capable of handling the job.

Other ongoing changes in Cameroon's public sector include:

♦ the definition of output factors to set up an evaluation system;

♦ increase in remuneration aimed at motivating personnel;

♦ decentralisation of the management of personnel;

♦ improvement in the system of communication between the public sector, economic operators and the civil society;

♦ computerisation of public administration.

THE GAMBIA

Country Profile

Location: The Gambia is the smallest country in West Africa. Apart from a stretch of coastline along the Atlantic Ocean, it is entirely surrounded by Senegal.

Capital: Banjul

Area: 10,689 sq km varying in width between 50km near the mouth of the river to 25km upstream and stretching 350km in length

Population: 1.3 million (estimate). The Madinka people comprise 42 per cent of the population, followed (in descending order) by the Fula, Wollof, Jola and Sarahuli. There is also a community of Akus (Creoles), descended mainly from Africans freed from slavery in the early 19th century.

Language: English is the official language.

Government: The Gambia became internally self-governing in 1963 and achieved independence in 1963. HM Queen Elizabeth II, represented by a Governor General, was Head of state until 1970, when following a referendum, a republican constitution was introduced. The 1970 Constitution also enshrined the strong traditional structures by giving a voice in the legislature to the chiefs.

Economy: The main features of the Gambia economy are its small size, narrow economic base, heavy reliance on agriculture and limited number of cash crops, mainly groundnuts. The agriculture sector represents a major determinant of economic activity both in terms of output (about 22 per cent of GDP) and employment (about 70 per cent of the total labour force). Tourism is another important sub-sector in terms of employment and foreign exchange earning, accounting for 10 to 12 per cent of GDP

Quality and Productivity Concerns in the Public Sector

The Gambia Public Service is structured in the same way as those of other commonwealth countries, having inherited that structure from the British colonial administration. The public service, though small in comparative standard, is dynamic with mostly hardworking and dedicated staff.

A major concern of the National Public Service is the need to develop a Careers Assessment Programme (CAP) for young, bright, ambitious and hardworking professionals. This would enable their talent and potential to be identified early so as to give them specialised and accelerated training, special assignments and a wide range of government experiences in preparation for competition for senior management positions. The goal is to retain such professionals in the service by giving them recognition, challenging work, a competitive working environment and proper performance-based incentives.

Public Sector Reform Issues

The Gambia has developed several national development policy frameworks that have assessed the country's development challenge from all angles – economic, social, political – and have set forth an overall vision, goals, priorities and strategies. These include the Vision 2020, the Programme for Sustained Development, Economic Management Capacity Building and Strategy for Poverty Alleviation. The main challenge for the government is to implement these national policies at the macro and sectoral levels in a sustainable manner while developing and sustaining the necessary human and institutional capacity to do so. The public service is, therefore, required to provide the necessary human and institutional capacity as well as create and sustain the enabling environment for these policies to be implemented successfully.

Thus, the Vision 2020 programme, which was launched in 1996, articulates the following public sector management strategy:

- The public sector shall re-organise institutional arrangements and encourage a spirit of management as opposed to mere administration. In the light of new relations to be forged with the private sector, a more efficient and effective civil service shall be achieved through constant reviews of public sector management and human resource development.

To address the vital issue of human capacity building in the public sector, training opportunities have been offered by donor countries and other international organisations. The government has also built training institutes for school leavers to be trained locally. The University of the Gambia was opened in 1999 to widen the opportunities already available in the higher education sphere.

Significant sector-based changes have been implemented. For instance, following a series of workshops on the way forward for the tourism industry, the Department of State for Tourism and Culture and stakeholders in the industry have adopted recommendations and an action plan to ensure that the government is committed to the revitalisation of the industry. In order to achieve this goal, the following objectives were advanced:

♦ improve the quality and presentation of the country's tourism product;

♦ explore and develop new markets;

♦ improve Gambia's image in existing markets;

♦ develop infrastructure in the department.

Strategies to achieve the above objectives include the provision of up-to-date information in the form of brochures, leaflets, posters and internet access in all Gambian embassies and tourist offices abroad. The government has taken the lead to create an enabling environment for tourism to thrive as well as provide adequate incentives to qualified investors. Some of the actions recommended in the National Tourism Policy 1995-2000 have already been implemented. These are the establishment of the National Tourism Authority, the repeal of the Tourism Act, and adopting a new image, a new logo and slogan.

Another significant reform measure is the decentralisation of the local government system. This takes cognisance of a primary objective of the country's National Governance Programme which seeks to ensure that the government exists to serve the electorate and that people's participation in development is guaranteed. Decentralisation is specifically provided for in the 1997 Constitution. The decentralisation of the local government system is, therefore, aimed at increasing local participation in decision making. This is being implemented through a two-pronged approach. First is the de-concentration of central government functions to the divisional level, for example, the establishment of Divisional Health Teams and

Regional Education Offices. Second is the transfer of responsibility for devolved functions and associated authority, power and resources to autonomous elected local government authorities. The transferred functions are aimed at improving the quality of municipal services such as waste disposal, local tax collection, provision of secondary roads, public markets and car parks, recreation and schools.

GHANA

Country Profile

Location: Ghana is situated on the west coast of Africa and is bounded in the north by Burkina Faso, in the west by Côte d'Ivoire, in the east by Togo and in the south by the Gulf of Guinea.

Capital: Accra

Area: 239,460 sq km

Population: 18.3 million (1997 estimate). Most of the population is concentrated in the southern part of the country with the highest densities occurring in urban areas and in cocoa-producing areas.

Language: English is the official language with a further eight main national languages.

Government: Ghana achieved independence in 1957 and became a republic in 1960. In 1992, after over a decade of military rule, the Provincial National Defence Council handed over the administration of the country to an elected government with constitutional rule and a multiparty parliamentary system.

Economy: The long term vision for Ghana is to systematically reduce poverty and promote sustained accelerated growth and equitable development so that by 2020, Ghana will have achieved a balanced economy and a middle income country status. The Economic Recovery Programme (ERP) of Ghana was initiated by the government in 1983. Under the ERP and the complementary Structural Adjustment Programme (SAP), the government introduced fundamental reforms to improve and strengthen the macro-economic framework of the country. Although Ghana's GDP has grown more rapidly than that of most sub-Saharan African countries, the relatively high population growth and lapses in public sector management have contributed in retarding progress towards achieving the desired leap in the living standard of the ordinary Ghanaian.

Quality and Productivity Concerns in the Public Sector

The long period of economic decline in Ghana in the 1970s and early 1980s led to lower productivity in the civil service. It suffered from steadily declining wages, overstaffing in non-critical occupational grades, and the flight of skilled civil servants abroad. To improve the performance of the civil service and strengthen its capacity for policy implementation, the government, in collaboration with donor partners, launched the Civil Service Reform Programme (CSRP), which lasted from 1987 to 1993. Although significant success was achieved, a review of the reform programme revealed some factors that had reduced its effectiveness as a change management mechanism. Notable among them was that the original terms of reference was relatively narrow in scope, not sufficiently comprehensive, and not tied to a well understood policy framework.

Public Sector Reform Issues

To address the weakness of the CSRP, the Civil Service Performance Improvement Programme (CSPIP), developed by local reformers, was launched in March 1995. It is a major component of the National Institutional Renewal Programme (NIRP) which has oversight responsibility for all public sector reforms. The overall goal of the CSPIP is to develop the capacity and efficiency of the civil service and all its constituent institutions. Specifically, the programme seeks to:

- encourage all civil service institutions to discharge their functions effectively in a transparent, competent, accountable and cost effective fashion;

- ensure that all civil service institutions take better care of their assets and resources, and utilise them more effectively and judiciously;

- improve responsiveness to the needs of the private sector and contribute towards supporting high national growth efforts;

- evolve an efficient, compact and well managed civil service which will deliver 'value for money' services;

- ensure that Ministries, Departments and Agencies (MDAs) develop strategic plans which specify their output and service delivery targets against which performance can be monitored and measured;

- motivate civil servants towards results-oriented practices and performance, and justify the linkage with appropriate pay and incentive schemes.

Key elements of CSPIP are the formation of Capacity Development Teams (CDT), administration of institutional Self Appraisal Instrument (SAI), conduct of

Beneficiary Surveys, organisation of Diagnostic workshops and Performance Improvement Plan (PIP) validation workshops, and PIP implementation/monitoring. A total of 180 institutions went through the first cycle of reforms which ended in August 2001 and are implementing their PIPs.

One dimension of the Civil Service Performance Improvement Programme is gender mainstreaming in the public service. Like many countries worldwide, the majority of senior management are men. Gender inequalities have mitigated against the ability of women to take decisions that affect their economic and social wellbeing. Initial actions to ensure proper integration of women include a policy statement on affirmative action for the promotion of equality of rights and opportunities for women nationwide and more recently, the creation of a Ministry for Women's Affairs.

Also a Gender Secretariat has been established at the Office of the Head of Civil Service with responsibility for implementing programmed change actions for gender mainstreaming in the public service, that is, to monitor, evaluate and promote equal rights and opportunities for women in the public service. The secretariat is also tasked with developing and promoting gender policies, receiving and addressing gender concerns, and facilitating accelerated training for women in the public service. Furthermore, focal persons have been designated as Women's Desks Officers in all Ministries, Departments and Agencies (MDAs), Regional Coordinating Councils (RCCs) and District Assemblies (DAs).

Another critical area of reform is the Public Service Commission. With the coming into force of the 1992 Constitution, the Public Service Commission which is responsible for the efficient performance of all the public service, has had its scope of operation considerably enlarged. It is now charged with the promotion of efficiency, accountability and integrity in the public service, provision of guidance for the public service as a whole, establishment of standards and qualifications, scheme of service and method for the evaluation of performance, ensuring justice and equity in recruitment, posting, transfer, redundancy and disciplinary matters, and establishing proper standards of grading of posts, terms and conditions of service throughout the public service.

In all cases, the Public Service Commission's involvement relates to the following three major functions: supervisory, regulatory and consultative functions. In order to enable the Commission effectively discharge its functions under its expanded role, the fundamental structure and job contents of the Commission have been reviewed. For example, a new organisational chart was designed to replace the existing one. The main features of the chart include the re-designation of the old 'schedules' to 'Divisions', the re-alignment of activities into main tasks to address weaknesses arising from the practice where almost all heads of Divisions performed functions that have to do with appointments, promotions, etc.

Based on the belief that the attainment of the goals and objectives of the Commission depends largely on the calibre of workers that are available and how they are organised and motivated to attain these goals, the Human Resource Development Division regularly draws up long and short term training programmes for the staff. The training programmes are to enable the staff to understand and be totally committed to the plans and visions of the Commission, to develop their skills and acquire modern management tools in order to meet the needs and expectations of the clients. Furthermore, the Commission has made efforts to provide staffing to an optimal level, although considerable difficulty has remained with regard to the Commission's attempts to recruit specialist staff for its technical Division.

Other reform programmes in the public sector include:

- **Public Financial Management Reform Programme (PUFMARP):** This seeks to evolve a performance budgeting system which measures output in relation to the cost of inputs. It also seeks to support this with improved accounting and auditing systems to ensure judicious use of limited financial resources. The ultimate goal is to devolve greater autonomy in financial administration to Ministries, Departments and Agencies through properly co-ordinated mechanisms which ensure financial accountability. The programme is managed by the Ministry of Finance.

- **Public Sector Income Policy and Administration:** This exercise is concerned with the development of the policy base, guidelines and imperatives that will inform the salary structures of a new pay policy. It is expected that if a universal salary structure and a unified public service work force are put in place and compensation is enhanced in the process, the necessary environment would be created for the public service to live up to its performance capability as envisaged under Ghana Vision 2020.

- **Decentralisation Policy (Administrative Reforms):** The reforms are designed to transfer political and administrative authority to District Assemblies which are the political authority at the level of the local government system. It is anticipated that empowering the people at the grassroots will enable them to improve delivery of services and living conditions at the local level. This programme is managed by the Ministry of Local Government and Rural Development.

MALAWI

Country Profile

Location: Malawi is a landlocked country in Southern Africa. It is bordered to the north and north east by Tanzania, to the south east and south west by Mozambique and to the west by Zambia.

Capital: Lilongwe

Area: 118,484 sq km

Population: Malawi has a population of around 10 million people from several ethnic groups. The predominant ethnic groups are the Chewas in the central region; Yaos, Lomwes and Senas in the southern region; and Nkhondes, Lambyas, Tongas, Tumbuka and Ngonis in the northern region. About half of the population live in the southern region.

Language: Chichewa is the national language; English is the official language.

Government: Malawi attained independence in 1964. After 30 years of one political party hegemony, the country now prides itself on a multiparty system of government. The multiparty political dispensation is guided by a new constitution which provides for the existence of a bicameral legislature consisting of a National Assembly and a Senate.

Economy: Malawi is an agricultural country with about 90 percent of the population employed in that sector. Agriculture contributes around 40 per cent of the Gross Domestic Product (GDP) and accounts for almost 85 per cent of the country's export earnings.

Quality and Productivity Concerns in the Public Sector

In Malawi, the following are the leading quality and productivity concerns in the public sector:

- **Political barriers:** Managerial issues including efficiency have not always been accorded high priority by either political or career executives. Politicisation of the senior ranks has often hampered the ability of the bureaucratic process to meet the challenges of the day.

- **Public goals and objectives:** These are often multiple, vague and sometimes conflicting, making it difficult to concentrate resources on critical elements.

- **Organisation structures:** Confusing organisational structures also constrain productivity. During the past two decades, both the number and size of ministries/departments have grown dramatically. In the process, complex organisational structures with multiple layers of line and staff offices and numerous administrative regulations have emerged. This increases the time it takes a ministry/department to carry out the routine and necessary steps to execute their programme mission.

- **Budget process:** The budget process in Malawi has been another powerful barrier to public sector productivity. Government ministries and departments have traditionally failed to justify their budget requests or to defend proposed staff increases on the basis of documented workload analyses or work measurement standards. In reality, productivity measurement data has been rarely used to justify and link staffing requirements to projected funding levels.

- **Poor personnel policies and practices:** Public management is also limited by a myriad of often unnecessary, obsolete and contradictory rules and regulations, old fashioned selection procedures, outdated job designs and classifications, and unrealistic and demoralising remuneration packages.

- **Lack of authority and autonomy:** Compared with those in the private sector, state sector managers enjoy less authority and autonomy in financial and personnel decisions.

- **Lack of information:** One of the major constraints to productivity improvement in the Malawi Civil Service is the inadequate system for collecting data and producing information that can be used in making and implementing decisions.

Public Sector Reform Issues

With the ongoing reform programme in the public sector, a number of changes are taking place. Below are some of the prominent changes:

- **Functional review:** This is aimed at redefining the roles and functions of government with a view to hiring off functions not considered a necessary part of government.

- **Rationalisation:** The goal is to control the size and growth of government employment so that over-staffing is eliminated and government can ultimately afford to competitively compensate its employees.

- **Job evaluation and salary restructuring:** This is aimed at rationalising and enhancing civil service pay by eliminating the distortions and anomalies that have crept into the system and by improving total compensation at all levels.

- **Decentralisation:** The purpose of this is to rationalise central and local government linkages and to facilitate further transfer of authority, responsibilities and resources to the districts.

- **Personnel, Payroll and Pension Integration (PPPI):** This involves the integration of records for efficiency, aimed at improving the processing of pensions and the establishment.

- **Medium Term Expenditure Framework (MTEF):** This is a strategic approach to public expenditure planning which provides a framework for allocating resources in line with government policies and priorities.

MAURITIUS

Country Profile

Location: Mauritius is a group of islands in the south west of the Indian Ocean, east of Madagascar. Mauritius includes the main island of Mauritius and the offshore islands of Rodrigues, Aglega Islands and the Cargados Carajos Shoals.

Capital: Port Louis

Area: 2,040 sq km (including other islands).

Population: Mauritius has a population of approximately 1.2 million, comprising Indo-Mauritians (66 per cent), people of mixed European and African origin (31 per cent) and Sino-Mauritians (3 per cent). Mauritians are descendants of immigrants from the Indian sub-continent, Africa, Europe and China.

Language: English is the official language; Creole is the mother tongue of many Mauritians and French is also widely spoken.

Government: Mauritius became an independent state in 1968 and acceded to the status of Republic within the Commonwealth in 1992.

Economy: The economic history of Mauritius reflects distinct phases of development strategies. Mauritius was a monocrop economy based on sugar until independence in 1968 when its export-oriented industrialisation process took off. The Export Processing Zone was designed to encourage the setting up of labour intensive export-oriented manufacturing enterprises, concentrated mostly on textile-related products. The tourism sector projected itself in the 1970s and 1980s as a serious economic pillar of growth. Since the 1990s, the focus has been on the service sector, especially on international financial services driven by offshore and freeport activities.

Quality and Productivity Concerns in the Public Sector

The government of Mauritius is the largest single employer in the country with around 85,000 employees in the public service, comprising local government bodies, public corporations and other state agencies. The entire public service accounts for about 20 per cent of the total labour force. The civil service, as the executive arm of government has increased in size to cope with the expansion of government activities, but without a well-structured pattern. The Mauritian civil service currently faces the following challenges, among others:

- globalisation and technological improvements, which have sharpened competition, exert pressure on the civil service to adopt new management practices to be more competitive;

- the expansion of new services in the civil service calls for new skills and knowledge;

- high public expectations for quality service;

- tasks and responsibilities are not always clearly defined;

- public officials are not paid or promoted on performance basis nor are they necessarily dismissed because of poor performance.

Public Sector Reform Issues

The Action Plan 2001-2003, launched in 2001, has the theme 'Towards the modernisation of the Civil Service'. It contains 13 strategic objectives ranging from re-engineering and restructuring of the public service, training and distance learning to advocating a caring, customer-oriented approach and quality culture. Task forces have been set up to focus on the following areas: performance management, human resource management/development, re-engineering and restructuring of the civil service, quality management and financial management. Other major areas of public sector reform in Mauritius include:

- **One-Stop-Shops:** The government has set up one-stop-shop facilities to cut down on bureaucratic delays and to simplify and speed up the processing of applications for licences, investment projects, work permits, etc.

- **Information Technology:** Various institutions have been set up to foster the development and growth of information technology and computer related services as well as training institutions in information technology. All ministries and government departments have their own websites on the internet. Several ministries have computerised their systems such as the Treasury Accounting System, the Contributory Pension System of the Ministry of Social Security;

the Customs Management System; the Income Tax Payment System and the Government Payroll System. Some 20 other computerisation projects are in the pipeline.

♦ **Training:** The government continues to place great importance on training in an effort to enhance the human resource potential in the public sector. The University of Mauritius, the Mauritius Institute of Education, the Mauritius Institute of Health, the State Informatics Training Company and the Mauritius Institute of Public Administration and Management all contribute to the training efforts. The government in collaboration with the above named institutions runs training schemes for public officers with specialisation in areas such as public administration and management, public finance, social studies, teaching, educational management, paramedical studies, information technology, secretarial and office management studies.

♦ **Public Sector Initiatives for Excellence Project (PSIE):** Based on the Singaporean model of Total Quality Management (TQM) strategy, the Ministry for Civil Service and Administrative Reforms launched the PSIE project in April 1999. Some of the components of the PSIE being implemented are the ISO 9000 Standards, Work Improvement Teams strategy, Vision and Strategic Planning, and Staff Suggestion Schemes.

♦ **Introduction of Standard Quality ISO 9000:** In April 1998, a pilot project for the introduction of ISO 9000 standards was started in the following five areas of the civil service with a view to improving the quality of service provided to customers: the Cabinet Office (Prime Minister's Office); the Subramania Bharati Eye Hospital, Moka (Ministry of Health and Quality of Life); the Arrival Terminal of the SSR International Airport (Civil Aviation Department); the Passport and Immigration Office (Prime Minister's Office); and the Service Counter of the Curepipe Post Office (Postal Services). Consultants from Scotland and Singapore have conducted training, awareness campaigns and system review. They have also provided guidance in the wri-ting of procedures and quality manuals, and internal quality audit exercises.

♦ **Code of Ethics for Public Officers:** This sets out the standards of correct behaviour expected of public officers. It provides guidelines based on values of integrity, honesty, impartiality and objectivity for appropriate conduct of public officers in a variety of contexts. It also informs members of the public what to expect of public officials in conduct and attitude when dealing with them. The objectives of the code are to promote responsible behaviour by helping public officers understand their responsibilities and obligations; instil a high sense of conduct and behaviour in the public service; promote a new culture through the adoption of moral values based on equity, fairness and accountability.

MOZAMBIQUE

Country Profile

Location: Mozambique lies along the eastern coast of Southern Africa and borders Tanzania, Malawi, Zambia, Zimbabwe, South Africa and Swaziland.

Capital: Maputo

Area: 799,380 sq km

Population: Mozambique has a population of nearly 15.7 million (1997 census).

Language: Portuguese is the official language; English is widely spoken.

Government: Mozambique became independent in 1975. The country is a unitary, multiparty democracy.

Economy: Mozambique's economy is recovering after nearly two decades of war and underdevelopment. In 1987, the government launched an Economic and Social Rehabilitation Programme, resulting in fundamental reforms of the system and the implementation of a market economy. The basic goal of the programme is to achieve financial stability at national and international level, and to reactivate the economy in a sustainable form.

Quality and Productivity Concerns in the Public Sector

Until recently, structural economic issues and post-war national reconstruction relegated concern with the productivity and quality of public service management to secondary importance. But it is increasingly clear that without focused and effective public service delivery, investment and improvements in basic human development will be hindered. Excessive political and administrative centralisation, lack of planned and rational management of human resources, the failure to apply rules for the recruitment and selection of civil servants, together with defective academic and professional training, have all led to urgent measures to reverse this situation.

Public Sector Reform Issues

The changes occurring in Mozambique's public sector aim to:

♦ improve the quality of public service and raise its image;

♦ dignify civil servants and improve their work conditions;

- break the centralised chain of command and delegate authority to lower levels that are closer to the public;

- improve the quality and qualifications of civil servants, and change behaviours and attitudes;

- clarify roles, responsibilities and functions of ministries and staff, eliminating redundant functions and activities.

Establishing the human foundation is the focal issue in order to make the management of change process viable and to consolidate it. This has meant:

- working to change the current pyramid of the public service, by increasing the number of staff at middle or higher levels so as to give the government the capacity to analyse, plan and develop national policies. This change will be achieved through training, recruiting and attracting staff of middle or higher academic qualifications and by introducing incentives for the higher levels.

- providing adequate remuneration for civil servants, linked to long term (career) and in some cases, short-term (target-based) performance incentives.

- decentralising structures and systems in order to move decision making closer to regions and communities served so as to increase managerial flexibility.

- promoting professional responsibility, improving ethics and a culture of 'service to the public' within the public service.

Since 1990 much has been done. Political reform including constitutional change formally redefined the role of the party and of the government vis-à-vis state institutions, the civil society and the private sector. Restructuring of the central government included the consolidation of ministries and clear specification of roles, functions and accountability. A number of state and public utility enterprises such as electricity, water, transport, telecommunications were privatised.

The organisation of the civil service included the clarification and promulgation of rules and terms of service, the introduction of standard job classifiers and a uniform salary structure, introduction of standard personnel files and computerised personnel data base for planning purposes.

A committee of ministers has been created to co-ordinate the reform of the public sector in Mozambique, which proves that at higher level there is now a political commitment to the need for change. The president of the committee is the Prime Minister. The deputy is the Minister of Public Administration and there is a technical team that advises the committee.

NAMIBIA

Country Profile

Location: Namibia shares boundaries with the South Atlantic Ocean on the west, Angola to the north, Botswana to the east and South Africa to the south. The Caprivi Strip, a narrow extension of land in the extreme north-east, connects it to Zambia.

Capital: Windhoek

Area: 824,269 sq km (including Walvis Bay 1,124 sq km)

Population: 1,613,000 (1997). The Ovambo and Kavango together comprise 60 per cent of the total population. Other groups are the Herero, Damara, Nama, Caprivians, San (Bushmen), Basters, and the 'Cape Coloureds'.

Language: The official language is English. Oshivambo is spoken throughout most of the north. Afrikaans is widely spoken.

Government: Namibia became independent in 1990. The constitution pro-vides for a multiparty democracy in a unitary state.

Economy: Namibia's economy is driven by export-focused mining and fish processing. Since independence, exports of diamonds, uranium, zinc and fish products have grown strongly. Rural people, however, remain largely unaffected by these activities and, according to UN reports, Namibia has one of the most uneven distributions of income in the world. The government's current objectives are to raise per capita income, to develop the private sector and to encourage manufacturing activities and tourism. It is also committed to restraining growth in public spending.

Public Sector Reform Issues

Concerted effort towards quality and productivity improvements in the country's public service led to the establishment of the Efficiency and Charter Unit (ECU) in the Office of the Prime Minister. Major developments are underway through this Unit and other existing structures to create awareness and promote a productive and quality conscious culture in the public service. To this end, a new salary grading system was introduced in April 1996; adequate and appropriate training programmes are initiated through the Department Public Service Management; strategic plans are developed for individual offices and ministries; and accounting officers and permanent secretaries are under tremendous pressure to exercise and practise sound operational and financial management in their respective offices/ministries. The Efficiency Charter Unit has developed customer charters for each office/ministry.

These customer charters clearly outline the basic principles of quality service and set the tone for a move in the direction of improved productivity and quality.

However, it is evident that a major shift of focus towards quality, productivity and the operational efficiency of the public service is yet to take place at all levels of the public service. Major issues such as affirmative action and rightsizing/downsizing still dominate the agenda items in the public service reform process. Other issues being considered in the effort towards a complete organisational change in the country's public service include:

- a clear framework of performance objectives;

- linking budgets to outcome;

- creating an innovative culture of management;

- taking advantage of new technologies;

- training and developing the workforce;

- evaluation and redesign of the public service delivery systems;

- securing all-round commitment from all stakeholders;

- setting up appropriate monitoring and evaluations systems;

- creating a productive and quality conscious culture.

NIGERIA

Country Profile

Location: Nigeria is situated along the west coast of Africa. It lies on the Gulf of Guinea and shares borders with the Republic of Benin in the west, Niger in the north, Chad in the north east and Cameroon in the east.

Capital: Abuja

Area: 923,768 sq km

Population: Nigeria is the most populous nation in Africa. The country has a population of around 120 million drawn from some 250 ethnic groups with diverse cultures and religious backgrounds. There are three major ethnic groups, namely the Hausa in the north, the Yoruba in the west and the Igbo in the east. The urban population accounts for about 30 per cent of the population.

Language: English is the official language. Hausa, Yoruba, Igbo and over 200 other languages and dialects are spoken in different parts of the country.

Government: Nigeria attained independence in 1960. It has a multiparty democratic three-tier system: the federal or central level, the state level and the local government. The country has been under military rule intermittently for most of its independent years, culminating in 28 years of military rule since 1960. A democratically elected government assumed office in May 1999.

Economy: The dominant occupation is farming, but oil accounts for over 80 per cent of foreign exchange earnings. The country recently commenced the exportation of liquefied natural gas.

Quality and Productivity Concerns in the Public Sector

Nigeria, like many other developing countries, is faced with problems of heavy external debt, widespread unemployment, increasing level of poverty, low growth rate and low productivity. The challenge of reversing this trend lies heavily with the institutions for formulation and implementation of policies that will promote growth and good governance. When the elected civilian administration assumed office in May 1999, the President in his inaugural address expressed government commitment to:

- good governance;

- fighting corruption;

- re-energising and re-engineering the public service to make it an effective instrument for policy formulation and implementation;

- privatisation; and

- poverty alleviation.

In addition to the policy thrust of the administration, the leading concerns in the Nigerian public sector are:

- the impact and imperatives of globalisation;

- changing old bureaucratic rules and procedures so as to respond positively to the demands of a market-driven economy;

- improving institutional performance to achieve customer satisfaction;

- integrity, accountability and transparency in the conduct of government business;

- professionalism of the public service.

The major obstacles in the realisation of these ends are resistance to change, poor infrastructural facilities, poor communications systems, low level development in information technology, ethnic factors and divisive political forces.

Public Sector Reform Issues

The public sector in Nigeria has gone through a number of reforms with the aim of making it responsive to the changes in government policies. Of particular significance are the 1974, 1988 and 1995 reforms. To date, the 1974 reforms remain the most profound of them all. However, while the country implemented the aspect of the reforms regarding improved wages, the structural and systemic review aspects received less attention. The 1988 reforms, on the other hand, became infamous for politicising and polarising the public service and fostering abuse of the federal character principle in the appointment and promotion of civil servants. The 1988 Civil Service Reform Law was repealed in 1995.

Recent changes in the Nigerian public sector have involved the following measures:

◆ training and re-training of all levels of civil servants as well as political office holders (human and institutional capacity building);

◆ re-orientation of civil servants and the political leadership;

◆ re-structuring the public service machinery and addressing the issue of right sizing;

◆ rationalisation of executive agencies and merging organisations that perform similar functions;

◆ job evaluation and performance management;

◆ staff audit to determine actual size of the service, actual personnel cost and remove ghost workers (this exercise is being carried out by independent auditors);

◆ introduction of new annual performance evaluation system which involves target setting;

◆ review of the civil service rules and financial regulations;

◆ greater emphasis placed on merit in the appointment and promotion of civil servants;

◆ establishment of a National Privatisation Council under the chairmanship of the Vice President to vigorously pursue the privatisation policy of the administration;

◆ establishment of a Policy Implementation and Monitoring Unit with committees in various ministries and extra-ministerial offices to ensure the prompt and effective implementation of the budget;

- promulgation of Corruption and Allied Practices Act and establishment of a tribunal to try offenders as well as the empowerment of the Code of Conduct Bureau and Public Complaints Commission;

- establishment of one-stop-shop systems in the ports, investment promo-tion board and company registration sub-sectors;

- computerisation of many areas of government business;

- substantial increase in the remuneration of public officers;

- encouraging public-private sector partnership;

- creating an enabling environment for the growth of the private sector;

- empowering the management services office to install and monitor best practices techniques in all ministries.

SEYCHELLES

Country Profile

Location: The Republic of Seychelles lies in the western part of the Indian Ocean, north of Madagascar and 1,593km east of Mombasa, Kenya. It is an isolated archipelago made up of about 115 islands; and the main populated islands lie around 1,500 km off the Coast of East Africa. Many of the islands of Seychelles are coralline, spread over a very wide sea area and similarly quite remote.

Capital: Victoria

Area: The land area is 455 sq km but the country has a large maritime zone of more than 1.3m sq km.

Population: Seychelles has a population of less than 100,000. Majority of the population live on three main granitic islands, which are situated in the north of the archipelago. Mahe, the largest island, has about 88 per cent of the population. The remaining 12 per cent live primarily on Praslin and La Digue, two islands which lie close together, about 45 km away from Mahe.

Language: The official languages are Creole, English and French.

Government: Seychelles became independent in 1976. By its 1993 constitution, Seychelles is a unitary republic with a multiparty democracy. It has a unicameral parliament.

Economy: The small size of the country has in some respects facilitated development, while in other respects it has imposed certain challenges. There is a high level of concentration of certain economic activities which reflect the comparative advantage of the country. The tourism sector predominates. The bulk of domestic commodity exports relate to fish and fish products. This high level of economic concentration constitutes a dimension of the country's economic vulnerability. Land for suitable agricultural projects is scarce and must compete with housing and other infrastructure development.

Quality and Productivity Concerns in the Public Sector

At independence in 1976, the size of the civil service was less than 3,000 employees. By 1983, there were nearly 6,800 government employees and another 5,000 employees in parastatal organisations, making a total of some 11,800 public sector or 65 per cent of the total workforce at the time. The development priorities at the time were the building of new schools, hospitals, power stations and other basic infrastructure in districts throughout the country, thus decentralising services and making them more accessible to communities. At the time, the country was still able to secure long-term development assistance on terms made favourable by a number of factors including the prevailing Cold War environment.

A recent performance audit exercise undertaken by each ministry/department to review their activities highlighted the following weaknesses, in particular:

◆ visions and roles are not clearly defined;

◆ ◆high service standards are set, but there is inconsistency in upholding them;

◆ shortage of qualified manpower;

◆ no Public Service Code of Conduct in place to strengthen discipline and address issues of ethics; and

◆ the need to review and update the Public Service Orders, Rules and Regulations.

The education sector has been a major focus of attention of government since independence. Pre-primary education is not compulsory, but is freely available to all children from about the age of four for a period of two years. Virtually all families avail themselves of this provision. Primary education is compulsory and is freely available to all children from the age of six for a period of six years. Secondary education is compulsory for the first four years and is also freely available to all students from the age of 12 for a period of five years.

Further education and training is provided in a range of institutions. Again, the emphasis has been on access for all and is dominated by public provision. The majority of secondary school leavers (75 per cent) enter a full-time further education or training course on leaving school. Seychelles has no university. This is because the population is considered too small to supply viable course intakes. Generally, those wishing to continue their education at university level do so at overseas institutions.

Two principal factors define the particular difficulties faced by the education system of Seychelles:

- **Target Setting:** The outputs of any education system (the students) are more complex and varied than the outputs of other organisations. They also represent a 'cycle time' in excess of 10 years. The setting of objective and measurable targets is, therefore, complex and difficult.

- **Small Scale:** In a small society, the functions that have to be performed are generally independent of scale. For example, an examination system requires high quality examination papers to be set and this requirement is independent of whether there are 1,000 candidates or one million candidates. Carrying out the wide range of required functions, with a numerically limited staff (who must consequently be broadly competent and have little scope for narrow specialisation) presents particular challenges. This applies in all aspects of administrative support to the education institutions.

Public Sector Reforms Issues

There are two particular aims in the public sector in Seychelles. These are to improve service to the public by reducing response time and to improve coherence between various sectors of the public service in order to reduce duplication of efforts and functions. In this regard, a number of critical initiatives are being pursued, including:

- **Stimulating performance** – The government has undertaken a number of measures to enhance the efficiency of public sector organisations. These include an improved scheme of service, simpler and more flexible salary scales, and contract terms of employment for senior and chief executives whose pay is related to performance against agreed targets within the contract period.

- **Staff Development Unit** – A special Staff Development Unit was set up to co-ordinate training needs for the public sector and work in close collaboration with the ministry responsible for national manpower development.

- **Downsizing** – Efforts have been made to reduce the size of the public sector. In 1999, for example, government froze all vacant positions on the public sector nominal roll. Only when a Chief Executive could fully justify the need for a particular post, was it re-integrated into the nominal roll. The Ministry of Finance works in close collaboration with the Ministry of Administration to contain the growth of personnel emoluments.

♦ **Information technology** – Seychelles has been developing an electronic government system which links key public service functions (for example, salary payment, taxation, immigration, physical infrastructure data, land data, company registration, public utilities) into one coherent information network. Some of these systems include the Human Resources Information System (HURIS), payroll and PERSPLAN. HURIS is basically a computerised nominal roll of the public sector; contains all posts and is administered centrally. It indicates such information as the position, entry point of the post, salary range and post number. This is matched on a regular basis with the payroll of the organisation and any significant discrepancies are highlighted and rectified.

The payroll calculates the salary, allowances, etc of all public sector employees. It also contains information from HURIS and has a list of various allowances that can be paid. All normal allowances have to be paid through the payroll, thus eliminating payment of any bogus allowances. Similarly, the incidence of ghost workers is eliminated because every employee is allocated a post number and national identity number. PERSPLAN is a computerised database of an employee profile which contains the present and past positions held, academic qualification, training, leave entitlement, external interests, etc. This is normally held within the Division and updated regularly.

In recent years, the education sector has similarly undergone intensive reform in the following domains:

♦ Infrastructures (schools and other education institutions) have been rationalised. This involved the closure or re-designation of a few institutions, in parallel with the building of a few new schools and the extensive infrastructural development of all secondary schools. The purpose of this development was to ensure that the basic facilities of institutions matched real needs (rather than approximated to real needs). This emphasis on infrastructure has been general in Seychelles and is a national policy for national development.

♦ Accountability of further education institutions has been reinforced by placing them in positions of direct accountability to the ministries/industries which they serve. Previously, further education institutions was managed by the Ministry of Education. Many are now managed by their 'parent ministries' and are accountable to these ministries/industries.

♦ All management structures of the Ministry of Education have been revised. This included both school management and central ministry management. The focus has been on accountability and effectiveness in supporting schools and students themselves.

◆ Quality assurance has been strengthened with the creation of a Quality Assurance section which focuses on the effectiveness of schools.

◆ An Information Technology master plan for the education sector has been produced. The issues of information technology in both the teaching/learning/distance education process and administration of the education system are seen as crucial in the short and long term.

SIERRA LEONE

Country Profile

Location: The Republic of Sierra Leone lies in West Africa and is bordered in the north by Guinea, in the south east by Liberia and to the south and west by the Atlantic.

Capital: Freetown

Area: 71,740 sq km

Population: The country has a population of 4.5million, 35 per cent of whom live in the urban areas.

Language: English is the official language.

Government: Sierra Leone became independent in 1961 and is a multiparty parliamentary democracy.

Economy: Since the early 1980s, the economy of Sierra Leone has become very depressed despite the country's rich resource base. Civil war in neighbouring Liberia and its spread into Sierra Leone, particularly from 1995, further damaged the economy. The country has also been burdened by an economically counter-productive parallel (or unofficial) economy, which increased in the lawless conditions of civil war. Around 90 per cent of diamonds produced in Sierra Leone have been estimated to leave the country illegally, and cash crops in the fertile south and east have also been smuggled out. The cost of maintaining a large army and bringing in foreign troops put a further strain on the economy.

Public Sector Reform Issues

The pervasive weaknesses in the public sector is explained by a number factors prominent among which are the lack of well articulated recruitment policies, poorly motivated and uncommitted civil servants arising from unfavourable reward systems and conditions of service, prevalence of non-meritorious promotion systems and the over-centralisation of government operations and institutions.

The civil service has also experienced a significant growth in size which also explains the constraints of managing it. Furthermore, the institution has suffered from a dearth of proper career paths, stemming from the ad hoc implementation of recruitment and training policies and programmes. This has been responsible for the lack of expertise and direction in the entire operations of the civil service.

In October 1998, a pilot diagnostic study was completed in four existing ministries – the Ministries of Education, Youth and Sports; Energy, Works and Technical Maintenance; Internal Affairs and Local Administration; and Trade, Industry and Transport. The study, carried out by a joint team of British and Sierra Leonean Management specialists, was to determine the dimensions of the problems faced by the public sector with a view to making preliminary recommendations for restructuring the ministries concerned. Subsequently, the UK Department for International Development (DFID) was approached to have the study extended to cover all ministries and for the urgent implementation of proposed recommendations.

The Office of the Establishment Secretary, also with the support of the DFID, has been converted to a Personnel Management Office to facilitate the development of the country's human resources. The eventual transformation is expected to result in a new personnel development and training policy, and resuscitation of the Civil Service Training College, which will cater for the middle and lower level staff development needs. The entire personnel records system in the civil service is being overhauled and computerised for proper record keeping.

A Pay and Grading Unit is being established in the Office of the Establishment Secretary to review the pay and grading system in the civil service. The system will link performance and rewards, and eventually with improved financial situation, salaries would be reviewed to make the civil service competitive with other sectors.

Similarly, a new personnel appraisal system is being developed to replace the outdated and stereotyped annual confidential reports. The new system will focus on performance and results for the purpose of awarding promotions and salary progressions. It is expected to encourage civil servants to be more committed to improving service delivery.

SOUTH AFRICA

Country Profile

Location: The Republic of South Africa has land borders with Namibia, Botswana, Zimbabwe, Mozambique and Swaziland; its sea borders are with the South Atlantic and Indian oceans. Lesotho is enclosed within its land area.

Capital: Pretoria (administrative), Cape Town (legislative), Bloemfontein (judiciary)

Area: 1,221,038 sq km

Population: The country's population of 43,336,000 (1997) is ethnically mixed. In 1995, blacks were estimated to constitute 76.5 per cent, whites 12.6 per cent, 'coloureds' (mixed race) 8.5 per cent and Asians 2.4 per cent.

Language: The official languages are Afrikaans, English, isiNdebele, Southern Sotho, Sesotho sa Leboa (Northern Sotho), siSwati, Xitsonga, Setswana, Tshivenda, isiXhosa and isiZulu.

Government: The 1990s brought an end to apartheid politically. South Africa's first non-racial and democratic elections were held in 1994.

Economy: Apartheid left South Africa with unequal distributions of income, distorted patterns of population settlement, imbalances in skills, low productivity and a large and inefficient bureaucracy. Furthermore, in the last decade of the old regime, prolonged recession (from low gold and other commodity prices, high expenditure on security forces, economic sanctions and disinvestment) led to weakening of the economic fabric. Removing this legacy and creating an equitable society with a dynamic economy is the government's major aim. The principal instrument for creating equality of opportunity include the Reconstruction and Development Programme (RDP), a massive house-building, and educational, health and infrastructure development programme.

Quality and Productivity Concerns in the Public Sector

Public sector reform in South Africa is premised on the following themes: improving the monitoring and evaluation of capacity on government initiatives, strengthening management capacity, improving quality of service, improving people management, and maximising the opportunities that technological advances present for e-government. Many decades of apartheid rule brought about gross skills inequalities on racial and gender bases. Efforts to drive implementation and service delivery are often not optimised because of the duplication of efforts amongst the agencies/departments.

The White Paper on the Transformation of the Public Service (WPTPS) of 1997 identified the following priority needs:

♦ rationalisation and restructuring to ensure a unified, integrated and leaner public service;

♦ institution building and management to promote greater accountability and organisational and managerial effectiveness;

♦ representativeness and affirmative action;

♦ transforming service delivery to meet basic needs and redress past imbalances;

♦ human resource development;

♦ employment conditions and labour relations;

♦ the promotion of a professional service ethos.

A major feature of the political struggle in South Africa was the progressive erosion of all forms of authority, especially that of the state. This was most marked in the field of education where schools were major sites of struggle. The Soweto uprising in 1976, the schools' unrest in 1979 and again in 1985-1986 illustrate the point. In this vein, there was a concomitant rejection of quality assurance by most teachers and students because they were regarded as measures applied by the oppressors. Visits by school inspectors and subject advisers to schools were broadly rejected, the authority and leadership of school principals were challenged by teachers; indiscipline at many schools was the norm. By the same token, South Africa found itself isolated from the rest of the world for so long that the large majority of South Africans were cut off from models of quality.

Some of the resultant ills in education highlighted in the research findings of the President's Education Initiative (PEI) Research Project of 1999 are as follows:

♦ conditions in schools in which the PEI studies were conducted stray far from those conducive to learning for substantial periods of time;

♦ of the 191 possible tuition days, in some cases 170 were lost through a whole host of external factors like registration of learners at the beginning of the year, slow start to subsequent terms, examination preparation, writing and marking, union meetings, strikes, pay days, memorial services, athletics and music competitions, district and regional meetings;

♦ divergent attitudes of teachers towards their work;

♦ low levels of teachers' conceptual knowledge;

- inability of teachers to practise learner-centred pedagogy;

- lack of structure to lessons and development of higher order skills.

Public Sector Reform Issues

Major reform issues in the public sector include:

- **Service Delivery Improvement:** The buzzword in South Africa today is service delivery, which is epitomised in the principles of *Batho Pele*, meaning 'people first'. The effectiveness of the public service is measured in its ability to respond to the needs of society, putting people first.

- **Multi-purpose centres:** Initiatives to provide one-stop service stations have been piloted in one of the Provinces (Northern Cape). The multi-purpose centres are an example of efforts to bring services to the people as encapsulated in the *Batho Pele* principles.

- **Strengthening management capacity:** As part of improving the quality of recruitment of managers, and providing for effective management development, all management positions in the public service are subjected to competency profiling. This has been complemented by the launching of a high level leadership programme – the presidential strategic leadership development programme designed to focus on areas such as strategic thinking and planning, human resource development, policy, research and knowledge management, service delivery, financial management, project management, communication and leadership.

With regards to the critical area of education, a number of improvements have been effected through the collective actions between the national and provincial education departments. The 19 education departments of the pre-democratic era, each of which had its own ethos and culture, were merged into one unified system. In the process, certain laws relating to schools and education were amended or repealed. New laws were enacted and a system of outcome-based education that seeks to reduce the gap between education, training and labour was introduced. Some of the changes in the education sector include:

- the quality assurance project which is a major effort towards quality improvement to assure that quality education permeates all aspects of education provision. The quality assurance project is based on four pillars, namely acceleration, learning site audits and reviews, programme and service reviews, monitoring learning achievement at key stages;

- the Batho Pele project which aims to change relationships between government and civil society;

- improvements in the capacity of governing bodies to govern schools effectively;

- instituting a 35-hour week for teachers;

- re-introduction of control mechanisms through which schools can be held accountable;

- reshaping the responsibilities of the circuit managers of schools and of the subject advisory service in order to provide support and development to schools;

- a development appraisal system for educators where the focus is on the quality of the pedagogical process, which is not judgmental, is more positively oriented and acknowledges people's strengths.

SWAZILAND

Country Profile

Location: The Kingdom of Swaziland is a landlocked country in Southern Africa, lying between the Republics of Mozambique and South Africa.

Capital: Mbabane

Area: 17,366 sq km

Population: The country's population of 906,000 (1997) is almost completely homogeneous, having one ethnic group and one national language, siSwati.

Language: English and siSwati

Government: Swaziland attained independence in 1968. It is a monarchy with power vested in the King who appoints the Prime Minister and the Council of Ministers (cabinet). Political arrangements in Swaziland have largely been influenced by the factors of its homogeneity, with a tendency towards conservation of tradition, common values and rule by consensus. This has given the country some degree of stability and has allowed for steady economic growth. On the other hand, Swaziland has tended to resist change within its political structures despite a rapidly changing socio-economic environment.

Economy: Swaziland has had a good record of economic development with sound achievements in delivering expanded and improved services, without increasing the public debt. However, there is need to meet the emerging challenges of the international and regional environment. These include the fact that the country has experienced changes from large budget surpluses in the late 1980s and early 1990s, to budget deficits recorded in recent years. Its vulnerability lies in heavy dependence on soft drink concentrate and sugar cane, and on South Africa which provides imports, investment and employment.

Quality and Productivity Concerns in the Public Sector

In order for government's major initiatives to succeed, Swaziland requires an efficient, responsive and effective public service. Thus, in areas where the public sector appears to be weak and ineffective, initiatives are being taken to review and reform it. Five critical areas of concern in the public service have been identified: overlapping portfolio responsibilities, inadequate organisation and management, low productivity, unsatisfactory services, and the cost and size of the civil service. In the face of a less buoyant economy, there has been a trend of rapid expenditure growth, especially of public service remuneration which absorbs on average 45 per cent of total government revenue.

Public Sector Reform Issues

To address these concerns, the Public Sector Management Programme (PSMP) was introduced in 1995. The PSMP aims to:

- ♦ ensure that resource allocations reflect national priorities by conducting ongoing and systematic reviews of priorities, policies, procedures, struc-tures and resource allocations of ministries/departments in order to create a more responsive public service;

- ♦ improve the performance, productivity and effectiveness of the public sector within a sustainable budget;

- ♦ improve accountability and transparency of government expenditure and provide improved management information systems to ensure a more proactive budget management;

- ♦ look into ways to improve the efficiency in the collection of revenues;

- ♦ consolidate expenditure reduction measures, subventions to public enter-prises, non-governmental organisations and other government subvented organisations;

- ♦ examine ways to reduce the involvement of government in areas where the private sector can offer services more efficiently and cost effectively.

The Ministry of Public Service and Information presently has overall respon-sibility for co-ordinating the Public Sector Management Programme in the country. However, a special office of National Director for the PSMP was established and has the day-to-day responsibility for implementing the pro-gramme. This office is also responsible for initiating and supervising special surveys, studies or consultancies which may be required to investigate critical issues that impact on the performance of the public service. The following interventions under the PSMP address these challenges:

♦ **Cost and size study:** A study to examine the size and sustainable cost of the civil service is being embarked upon. The main objective of the study is to determine the levels and the direction of the required size of the civil service.

♦ **Review of the human resources management function:** Closely associated to the issue of the cost and size of the civil service is the question of how human resources, as a critical and costly resource to government, is being managed in the Swaziland Civil Service. A study to review the operations of the Service Commissions and all offices that have responsibility for human resources management in the civil service was completed in 2001. New and revised legislative, administrative and institutional frameworks were recommended. Once fully implemented, a modern approach to human resources management will be adopted, with revised and tighter systems and procedures to enhance both performance and productivity.

♦ **Management audit services:** While the cost and size study takes a strategic view of the organisation and management of the whole civil service, the management audit services investigates the current operations of each ministry and department to ascertain their policies, how they are structured and how effectively the ministries are delivering services to the people. In line with the government's poverty alleviation strategy, the studies also investigate and consider the possibilities for decentralising the provision of public services to the regions in the rural areas where the majority of the Swazis live.

Four projects specifically address improving service delivery within the civil service. These are:

♦ **Opinion survey of the public concerning service standards and quality:** An opinion survey to rate the quality of the public services citizens receive from the government will enable more focussed interventions to improve clearly identified public services.

♦ **Developing a policy framework for alternative delivery of public service:** The main purpose of this intervention is to develop an appropriate policy framework for the identification, examination, agreement and implementation of alternative modalities for providing public services.

♦ **Inculcation of customer care and customer service attitudes:** Customer care and customer service training commenced in 2002 for front-line service ers. In addition, service standards will be developed for these front-line government services to the public.

♦ Promoting public service ethics: Closely linked to the issue of customer care and customer service is the issue of public service ethics. To this end, a Public Service Charter is being developed.

In addition to the projects under the Public Sector Management Programme, there are a number of other complementary reform measures being undertaken. These include:

♦ **Information and Communications Technology applications:** The government recently prioritised the concept of adopting and applying modern information and communications technologies (ICT) to enhance, integrate and make more effective all government operations and services being offered to the public. This project is under implementation by the Computer Services Department of the Ministry of Finance.

♦ **Decompression of pay scales and the introduction of a new job evaluation system:** In order to address the issue of compressed salary scales and the arising brain drain from the Swaziland Civil Service, the government recently completed an exercise to move from a single pay scale to multiple pay scales, in a bid to generally decompress the salary scales. This exercise also updated all job descriptions and developed a new job evaluation system.

♦ **Computerisation of human resources information system:** This is an ongoing project of the Ministry of Public Service and Information aimed at computerising the human resources management system in order to enhance quick information retrieval and management decision making.

TANZANIA

Country Profile

Location: The United Republic of Tanzania borders on the Indian Ocean to the east, and has land borders with Kenya, Uganda, Rwanda, Burundi, the Democratic Republic of Congo(across Lake Tanganyika), Zambia, Malawi and Mozambique.

Capital: Dar es Salaam; the capital designate is Dodoma.

Area: Total area, including inland water and Zanzibar, is 945,090 sq km.

Population: The country has a population of around 31,507,000 (1997). Most of the people are of Bantu origin with some 120 ethnic groups on the mainland, none of which exceeds 10 per cent of the population. There are Asian and expatriate minorities.

Language: The official language is Kiswahili and is the language of teaching in primary schools. English is the second official language, the country's commercial language and the language of teaching for secondary schools and higher education.

Government: In 1964, Tanganyika and Zanzibar united as the United Republic of Tanzania. (Tanganyika attained independence in 1961 and Zanzibar in 1963 as separate countries.) Tanzania has a unicameral Union Parliament. The constitutional changes in the 1992 constitution introduced a multiparty system. The Zanzibar administration has its own President and a House of Representatives for legislation on domestic matters and, in practice, external trade.

Economy: Tanzania entered into independence with a severely underdeveloped economy and extremely limited infrastructure. In an effort to bring about rapid yet socially equitable development, it became an early proponent of African socialism. In the one and half decades following independence, the country made fairly impressive progress in economic and social development. GDP growth averaged 4.7 percent up to the mid 1970s. But thereafter, the impact of over-extension of direct government investments, management and control of the economy, with a restrictive policy regime, together with a series of external shocks, including a severe draught, the war against the Idi Amin regime in Uganda, and oil price hikes in the early 1970s and early 1980s, resulted in serious macro-economic imbalances. The economy stagnated; per capita income declined, severe shortages occurred and living standards plunged. The implementation of structural reforms has led to economic recovery. However, because of the deep decline in per capita income and the sharp erosion of living conditions before the initiation of reforms, widespread low incomes persist even as the economy recovers.

Public Sector Reform Issues

After the attainment of independence, the socio-political and economic philosophy as well as the policies that were pursued, radically redefined the role and functions of the government. This entailed extensive government involvement in all spheres of the country's economic and social services, and centralised public planning, control and delivery of these services. However, this extensive government involvement was ultimately inconsistent with sustainable economic growth, and the efficient and effective delivery of public services. After a decade of economic decline, the public sector was characterised by under-funding and overstaffing. Civil servants were increasingly demotivated because of, among other things, a decline in their real incomes, political interference in appointments and serious distortions and inequities in promotion. All of these, consequently, translated into a severe weakening of institutional and administrative capacity.

It was against this background that the government launched the Civil Service Reform Programme (CSRP) in 1991 with the fundamental goal to achieve 'a smaller, affordable, well compensated efficient and effectively performing civil service'. The objectives of the CSRP were to reduce the scope of government to affordable levels; rationalise the machinery of government; develop open, objective and competitive pay structure; decentralise non-core functions to Local Authorities, Executive Agencies, NGOs and the private sector; and improve the performance of civil servants.

The CSRP implementation focused on the restoration of the structural preconditions to support fiscal stabilisation measures including removal of ghost workers, staff retrenchment, rationalisation of the pay and grading system, reinstatement of establishment and payroll controls to bring employment and the wage bill under control. Second were institutional improvements, including a redefinition of the role of government, restructuring for organisational effectiveness and efficiency, and outsourcing certain services decentralisation of service delivery managerial capacity building.

The programme achieved impressive achievements in both areas, especially in terms of cost containment, rationalisation of the pay structure, training for redeployment of retrenched employees and structural and institutional reforms. However, in an active search for sustainable and better results, an in-depth and critical assessment of the programme concluded that there was still much to be done to translate the results into improved and quality services to the people of Tanzania. The assessment indicated that the future reform programme strategy would need to contend with the following issues:

◆   the vision and goals of the reform programme had remained remote to public interest;

◆   weak local ownership of reform goals and inadequate implementation responsibilities in ministries, departments and agencies (MDAs);

◆   unaffordable levels of public expectations;

◆   decline in public service capacity to deliver services;

◆   some elements of resistance to change;

◆   performance undermined by low pay;

◆   weak monitoring and evaluation of outputs and outcomes.

In response to these challenges, the government has opted for a more comprehensive programme with a longer term perspective – the Public Service Reform Programme

(PSRP). The programme, whose strategic theme is 'quality public services under severe budgetary constraints', aims at transforming the public service into an institution that has the capacity, systems and culture for client orientation and continuous improvement of services. This will require more than a decade of sustained reform efforts and the programme will be implemented in three phases:

- **Phase 1 (2000 – 2004), Installing Performance Management Systems:** This will focus on a process that will engage participants, including ministries and departments, in structural changes, and reinforce the changes in structure to redefine role within the management process. The expected outcomes for this phase include improvements in service standards in key sectors; smaller workforce and budget shifts from wage to non-wage expenditure; improved real pay for professional, technical and management; objectives and key result areas defined by all ministries; private sector participation in delivering some of the non-core government services; all appointments and promotions on a competitive basis; and customer-oriented public servants.

- **Phase 2 (2005 – 2008), Instituting a Performance Management Culture:** The goal will be to extend result-oriented management practices throughout the public service and to complete the transfer of most service delivery responsibilities to local authorities and local communities. This phase will also be geared to support the restoration of effective public financial management practice particularly by fostering closer linkages between budgets and performance objectives.

- **Phase 3 (2009 – 2011), Instituting Quality Improvement Cycles:** In phase 3, it is expected that a new culture in public management practices will have been internalised throughout the public service. Client orientation and accountability for results would become the norm. Furthermore, measures to increase public and business participation in policy formulation would be introduced.

UGANDA

Country Profile

Location: Uganda is a landlocked country in Eastern Africa and is bordered by Sudan, Kenya, Tanzania, Rwanda and the Democratic Republic of the Congo.

Capital: Kampala

Area: 236,00 sq km including 36,330 sq km of inland water.

Population: 20,791,000 (1997). About 66 per cent of the population consists of

Bantu peoples in the south, the rest of Nilotic peoples in the north, and a small Asian minority.

Language: English is the official language.

Government: Uganda gained independence from the United Kingdom in 1962. Its present constitution promulgated in 1995 provides that for a period of at least five years, elections are held under the movement system, whereby candidates stand as individuals to be elected on personal merit, and not as members of a political party. The movement system will continue beyond five years subject to endorsement by a referendum.

Economy: Agriculture is the most important sector of the economy, employing over 80 per cent of the work force. Coffee is the major export crop and accounts for the bulk of export revenues. Throughout the 1970s and the first half of the 1980s, Uganda went through a difficult period as a result of widespread mismanagement and civil strife. All of these undermined the economic as well as socio-political fabric of the society, including the public sector. However, since 1986, the government, with the support of foreign countries and international agencies, has acted to rehabilitate and stabilise the economy by undertaking currency reform, raising producer prices on export crops, increasing prices of petroleum products, and improving civil service wages. The policy changes are especially aimed at dampening inflation and boosting production and export earnings.

Quality and Productivity Concerns in the Public Sector

Over the years, the public service became bloated and unresponsive to the needs of the society mainly because it lacked the necessary skills and tools. Furthermore, the lack of emphasis on proper planning resulted in the duplication of roles in a number of areas, which meant that the few resources available were not optimally utilised. The situation was compounded by the poor terms and conditions of service that obtained in the public sector.

To illustrate, the Education Service forms a large proportion of the Uganda Public Service and is governed by the Education Service Commission (ESC). Among the leading quality and productivity concerns within the education sector are:

- the need to attract high calibre/quality personnel into the service;

- developing such personnel through capacity building, attractive remuneration and other motivating factors;

- developing the capacity of the local governments to fulfil their mandate with regard to the Education Service;

- keeping accurate records of vacancies within the service, qualified personnel and their deployment;

- efficient management of the payroll.

Public Sector Reform Issues

In 1989, the government embarked on the onerous task of reforming the public sector. The work began with the appointment of the Public Service Review and Re-organisation Commission to review the entire public sector and make appropriate recommendations to government. The commission submitted its report in September 1990 with a total of 255 wide-ranging recommendations, some of which the government has implemented over time. One such example is the rationalisation and re-organisation of ministries in order to eliminate duplication and non-economic utilisation of resources. Phase I of this process led to the reduction from a total of 33 to 22 ministries. In a later re-organisation, this number was further reduced to 17 ministries. The restructuring resulted in the reduction of the public sector from 320,000 persons in 1992 to about 167,000 persons in 1997. The workforce was reduced both through voluntary retirement and compulsory retrenchment.

In 1993, Uganda embarked on an extensive policy of decentralisation backed by legislation. This was later consolidated by the provisions of the 1995 Constitution which under Article 176(2) states inter alia that:

- the system of local government shall be such as to ensure that functions, powers and responsibilities are devolved and transferred from the govern-ment to local government units in a co-ordinated manner;

- decentralisation shall be a principle applying to all levels of local govern-ment and in particular, from higher to lower local government units to ensure people's participation and democratic control in decision making;

- there shall be established for each local government unit a sound financial base with reliable sources of revenue;

- appropriate measures shall be taken to enable local government units to plan, initiate and execute policies in respect of all matters affecting the people within their jurisdiction;

- persons in the service of local government shall be employed by the local government;

- the local governments shall oversee the performance of persons employed by the government to provide services in their areas and to monitor the provision of government services or the implementation of projects in their areas.

As a result of the decentralisation policy, districts now manage a separate personnel system but in conformity with terms and conditions prescribed by the Public Service Commission for the public service generally.

Prior to 1996, pay constituted both basic pay and allowances. In order to streamline pay and to simplify pay management, a decision was taken to consolidate pay into one package, thereby eliminating the categorisation of pay into basic pay and allowances.

The changes given below are embodied in the five-year comprehensive Public Service Programme launched by the government on 28 November 1997:

- introduction and implementation of results-oriented management and output-oriented budgeting to ensure value for money;

- revision of the performance appraisal instrument in line with the demands of the results-oriented style of management;

- revision of both the Public Service Act and Standing Orders to bring them in line with the current environment and demands of a new era of public service;

- introduction of written examinations as a method of assessment for recruiting persons into the public service and for promoting serving officers;

- divestiture by government from non-core functions which will lead to the creation of semi-autonomous executive agencies.

Changes in the individual sectors are taking place within the broad framework of public service reforms. For instance, as stated in the Education Strategic Investment Plan 1998 – 2003, the focus is on:

- expanding access to education, beginning at the primary level with the introduction of Universal Primary Education (UPE) in 1997, providing vocational opportunities at the post-primary level and seeking to achieve and maintain higher transition rates from primary to secondary level;

- enhancing the quality and relevance of instruction through further training and curriculum review and improvement;

- increasing equity by ensuring that public expenditure is shifted in favour of geographically and socially disadvantaged areas;

- enhancing the capacity of the District and Local Governments to enable them deliver educational services as well as supervise the private providers.

- ensuring that local authorities contribute to education by apportioning part of their revenue collection to the sector.

The Education Service Commission issues guidelines to District Service Commissions regarding recruitment into the Education Service at the primary school level, assists districts to develop the capacity to gradually take on the management of the secondary level through mutual consultation and sensitisation of all stakeholders, as well as scrutinises existing legislation to ensure that the laws are in line with the provisions of the Constitution.

Since effecting the Education Plan, there have been better records management through staff training and an improvement in physical facilities. The building of a data bank of education sector personnel, which is a long term project, has commenced. In-service programmes that allow teachers to study while they continue to teach, are conducted during school holidays. Serving teachers are granted study leave with pay to enable them undertake courses leading to higher qualifications. Regular workshops, seminars and other interactive forum are strongly encouraged and often centrally organised. Training of record managers has been co-facilitated by the Ministry of Public Service.

ZAMBIA

Country Profile

Location: Zambia is a landlocked country on the Southern African plateau and is bordered by Tanzania, Malawi, Mozambique, Zimbabwe, Botswana, Namibia, Angola and the Democratic Republic of Congo.

Capital: Lusaka

Area: 752,614 sq km

Population: The country has a population of 8,4788,000 (1997) with over 40 per cent of the population living in the urban areas.

Language: English is the official language; Bemba, Nyanja, Tonga, Lozi, Luvale, Lunda and Kaonde are main languages.

Government: Zambia gained independence in 1964. The constitution provides for an elected executive President, who is Head of State and Commander-in-Chief of the Armed Forces. The Vice President and the Cabinet are appointed by the President from the National Assembly, which is an elected body.

Economy: Zambia's main revenue generating activities are manufacturing, mining (copper and cobalt together account for 70 per cent of exports), and agriculture (which is the largest source of employment). Zambia is classified as a low income country. Since 1981, the country has been undergoing a major economic and social change within the broader framework of the IMF and World Bank sponsored Structural Adjustment Programme.

Public Sector Reform Issues

The need to change the role of government from direct provider to enabler is recognised universally as a route towards improved economic efficiency. Pushed by the national economic crisis, the government has increasingly sought to adopt and develop structures and values as well as redefine the role and functions of the public service to improve performance. In 1993, the government officially launched the Public Service Reform Programme (PSRP) designed to transform the public service into a leaner, efficient, cost effective, responsive and affordable organisation capable of delivering quality services, and providing an enabling environment for private sector and individual participation in national development.

The objectives of the PSRP include:

◆ to improve government capacity to analyse and implement national policies and perform its functions;

◆ to effectively manage expenditure to meet fiscal stabilisation objectives; and

◆ to make the public service more efficient and responsive to the needs of the populace.

To realise its objectives, the PSRP has three components:

◆ **Restructuring of ministries and provinces:** This component aims to steamline and rationalise the structures and operations of government ministries, departments, agencies and provinces to attain a leaner and less costly, but more efficient public service. It also aims to document, analyse and propose improvement to the planning, programming and budgeting systems of the public sector in order to improve fiscal discipline.

◆ **Management and human resources improvement:** This component has three main objectives:
    • to develop critical skills to enable senior civil servants more effectively manage the public service;

- to put in place an effective personnel evaluation instrument and management information system to enable the government effectively compile and manage data needed for personnel decision making;
- to improve the remuneration and conditions of service.

◆ **Decentralisation and strengthening of Local Government:** This is aimed at making local government in particular, and district government in general, more efficient, cost effective and responsive to the needs of local communities in the delivery of services, and to ensure that local government is adequately financed. The implementation of these components has culminated in notable improvements and changes in approaches, some of which are highlighted below: management audits of ministries and provinces to learn in detail about their current operations and asset base;

◆ strategic planning workshops to develop comprehensive organisational strategic plans;

◆ designing optimal organisation structures and determining appropriate staffing levels, and job descriptions;

◆ developing and implementing appropriate programmes to assist retrenched workers find alternative means of livelihood;

◆ streamlining planning, programming and budgeting activities to improve fiscal discipline;

◆ working out mechanisms to run some government activities as profitable autonomous operations or privatised units, and abolishing unproductive operations;

◆ developing and installing Performance Management Systems (PMS) and an Annual Performance Appraisal System (APAS) to replace the Annual Confidential Report (ACR) which denied the appraised the opportunity to know their strengths and weakness;

◆ strengthening the capacity of local training institutions to deliver the required training to support the public service;

◆ developing an instrument enabling the Public Service Management Division (PSMD) to maintain an accurate and up-to-date database on civil servants for use in making appointments to posts based on objective criteria, merit and performance; and

◆ developing work plans specifying expectations of performance.

ZIMBABWE

Country Profile

Location: Zimbabwe is a landlocked country on the Southern African plateau and bordered by Zambia, Mozambique, South Africa and Botswana.

Capital: Harare

Area: 390,634 sq km

Population: The country has a population of 11,682,000 (1998) with about 33 per cent of the population living in the urban areas.

Language: English, Shona and Sindebele are official languages.

Government: Zimbabwe gained independence in 1980. Recently Zimbabwe has experienced a wave of political violence, largely occasioned by the government policy in land redistribution. The growing seriousness of the situation threatens even the limited economic and social development achievements gained since independence.

Economy: Zimbabwe has a relatively diversified economy, with good infrastructure, well-developed manufacturing, a relatively strong financial-services sector, and mining. Agriculture is the foundation of the economy and the determining factor in its growth. Periods of rapid growth have been interrupted by agricultural stumps caused by drought. Government policy is focused on encouraging foreign investment and expanding exports.

Public Sector Reform Issues

In 1989, a report of the Public Service Review Commission stated: 'A young and inexperienced cadre of civil servants has, in a matter of years, managed to deliver services which earlier had been denied to large sections of the population, particularly in education, health care and agricultural services. But the public administration of Zimbabwe is now in need of reform and modernisation because its processes and procedures were designed to implement more modest government policies than those now in force.' Supporting its claim with evidence collected from the general public, local authorities and the private sector, the report went on to add that the public service was:

- over-sized, cumbersome and heavily centralised;
- managed by inexperienced senior staff;
- characterised by overlap and duplication of functions;

- secretive, lacking in transparency, and with poor communication of decisions and problems;

- inaccessible to the general public; and

- suffering from over-complicated rules and elaborate procedures.

The commission noted that these characteristics led to delays in service delivery and a lack of responsiveness to the needs of the general public, which resulted in a widening gap between the population and the public service. Based on the review of the Review Commission report and subsequent studies, the following broad objectives underpin the current public service reform programme:

- improve the mechanisms for policy formulation and co-ordination;

- introduce performance management to ensure better service delivery;

- improve conditions of service to retain competent skills and enhance morale and motivation;

- improve resource management through intensive reviews of management in all departments and agencies;

- upgrade basic management systems through staff training;

- restructure public expenditure through a rational process of labour deployment, structural reviews and decentralisation;

- reduce the size of the public service;

- set up and strengthen monitoring and support systems;

- introduce computerised Human Resource Information Systems and a government-wide Management Information System.

To achieve these objectives, the Public Service Commission, which is the key player in designing, implementing and monitoring the reform programme, has implemented or is in the process of implementing changes which are designed to overcome the deficiencies highlighted by the Review Commission. The key elements of this reform are:

- **Performance management:** This is in the process of being introduced into all the ministries by encouraging managers to shift their focus from mere compliance with rules and other controls to seeking ways of achieving the best possible results. In effect, managers are being required to do more with less resources and are being held accountable for results. All ministries have drafted mission statements and training in the concept of performance management has already been provided at the top three management levels in ministries. Institutional arrangements to sustain the system are being expanded and National Training Institutes are being strengthened to enable them to provide performance management training to middle and lower-level managers throughout the service.

- **Management Information System (MIS):** This is being designed to measure the performance of ministries and individuals against set goals and objectives or key result areas. The MIS will form a basis for reward, sanction and identification of training and development needs.

- **Improve job definition and reward:** A review and evaluation of job structures has been an important step in the reform. Re-organisation has enabled the service to streamline operations, introduce parallel progression, and rationalise the numerous allowances introduced as a way to retain staff. To implement the job evaluation exercise, a compensation survey was conducted aimed at improving conditions of service to provide enhanced rewards to experienced staff in those occupations which have presented problems in staffing.

- **Appraise personal performance:** A performance appraisal system has been introduced to replace the previous procedures which were primarily related to personnel functions and focused on promotability assessments. Consistent with an increased emphasis on rewarding achievement, this system focuses more on objective setting, measurable outcomes, training needs and continuous dialogue between managers and staff.

- **Decentralise decision making:** As a means of improving efficiency and enhancing accountability, the Service Commission has already decentralised to ministries a substantial amount of operational activities. Ministry head offices, in turn, are expected to decentralise a substantial amount of their functions to the provincial and regional levels.

ASIA

to the needs of a modern economy. It is seen as being more concerned with rules and procedures, and less concerned with action. This makes it difficult to meet the needs of its citizens for better quality services.

- **Too many roles:** It still does things that others could do better. The government is admittedly taking steps to divest itself of some of these functions, but is seen as doing so too slowly.

- ◆ **Too centralised:** Rural communities account for the bulk of the population, yet there is no effective local government with the capacity and resources to provide them with public services. Moreover, many centrally provided services are selective in their coverage.

- ◆ **Unaccountable and unresponsive:** Public servants are not held individually accountable for poor performance and delayed decisions. Government programmes are inadequately scrutinised for overall efficiency, appropriateness or cost effectiveness. Only a small number of public servants view responsiveness to citizens as a fundamental obligation. Governance is too personalised and decisions get taken only after personal intervention.

The citizens' dismal view of the public sector is corroborated by evidence from the aggregate picture. For example, the government's performance continues to be inadequate in terms of the level, quality and timeliness of its public investment programme. Despite availability of concessional funds, public investment continues to account for only eight to nine percent of the GDP and delays of several years in project completion are common. This situation is due to the weak implementation capacity of public institutions and the absence of adequate accountability regime. Also government capacity and ability to establish an effective enabling framework for private sector development is weak, thus undermining private sector investments, which has remained at low levels of growth and account for six to seven per cent of GDP.

The problems posed by the poor state of public services are accentuated by the rapid growth in demand. Bangladesh has one of the fastest urbanising rates in the world. The urban population soared from six million in 1974 to 22 million in 1991. This places enormous strain on an already hard pressed urban system, particularly in the electricity, water, sanitation, telephone and education sectors.

Public Sector Reform Issues

Since independence a number of commissions, some with donor assistance, have been set up to remodel the public sector in Bangladesh. In more recent times, the Public Administration Reforms Commission (PRAC) set up in 1996 recommended several reform measures with a view to increasing efficiency, quality, productivity, accountability and transparency of the public service. Some of the interim reform measures suggested by the commission have already been put in place.

Considerable efforts have been made to separate the judiciary from the administrative sector. New financial courts were established to handle cases arising under the recently enacted bankruptcy law as well as to pursue loan defaulters more effectively. The public accounting system has been redesigned and extensive training of accounts staff to implement the new system has taken place. The efforts made by donors to support institutional reforms, principally through technical assistance have had some limited success in strengthening individual institutions.

One notable feature of the current reform regime relates to revenue generation, specifically the work of the National Board of Revenue. This Board is an arm of the government responsible for domestic resource mobilisation. Reform issues in this sector may be summed up as follows:

◆ Job/tasks were redefined and the number of officials/supporting staff was accordingly rationalised to eliminate duplication of work and to ensure that there are no idle labour force.

◆ All officials and staff undergo on-the-job training to give them a better understanding of their duties and responsibilities and to provide them with any new skills and attitudes necessary to cope with changes in the system.

◆ There are regular staff meetings to promote better understanding.

◆ There has been a systemic change in matters of revenue collection. An example is the simplification of excise duty collection from physical to paper control. Under the Excise and Salt Act, 1944, excise duty used to be levied on industrial and some selected agricultural goods by physical supervision at the time of clearance of goods. As the base of excise duty grew, it became more difficult to operate as more officials and staff were needed and allegations of harassment of the duty payers and of tax evasion increased. A shift away from physical control (supervision) to paper control was, therefore, introduced so that excise duty can be assessed and paid, as per clear and simplified rules, by the industrialists without the physical presence of excise officials. The system has worked with good results. Service delivery has become faster, the number of tax evasions cases has dropped and revenue collection has increased.

BRUNEI DARUSSALAM

Country Profile

Location: Brunei Darussalam is situated in the south-east of Asia, bordering the South China Sea and Malaysia. It shares a common border with Sarawak, one of the two eastern states of Malaysia, which also divides Brunei into two parts.

Capital: Bandar Seri Begawan

Area: 5,765 sq km

Population: 307,000 (1997), 70 per cent of whom live in the urban areas, concentrated along the coast.

Language: The official language is Malay. English is widely spoken.

Government: Brunei became an independent sovereign state on 1 January 1984, and is a sultanate. The constitution provides for the Sultan as head of state, a Council of Succession, a Privy Council, a Council of Ministers, a Religious Council and a Legislative Council.

Economy: The discovery of petroleum and natural gas in the 1920s changed the economy of Brunei making it the country with the highest per capita income in south-east Asia. Oil and natural gas are the twin pillars of Brunei's economy and provide the country with most of its export revenues.

Quality and Productivity Concerns in the Public Sector

The public service is the largest employer in Brunei Darussalam, employing around 40,000 employees. has changed over the years from that of acting simply as service provider. With educational development which has resulted in the increase of more capable and qualified workers for most jobs, advancement in information technology which has led to a new working culture and environment, as well as sophisticated clients demanding quality service, the role of the public service has become that of regulator and facilitator. To keep up with its enormous and competitive challenges, various reform programmes have been designed over the years to enhance the efficiency of the public service. However, it has been observed that after a period of implementation, enthusiasm begins to wear off. This calls for a continual focus on activities of the reform programmes.

Public Sector Reform Issues

Over the years, the government through the Civil Service Institute and various ministerial and department training centres has introduced and conducted training programmes in various fields of management, administration, leadership, communications and information technology. These training programmes have led to a better understanding of organisational policy, new ideas and approaches in the various fields, and their implementation in real work situation.

As with other public services in the ASEAN region, the Brunei Darussalam Public Service has also introduced the following initiatives as part of the continuous efforts towards improving and monitoring the performance level of government agencies: Client's Charter (Brunei's Tekad Pemedulian Orang Ramai, TPOR);

- Civil Service Excellence Award (Brunei's Anugerah Cemerlang Perkhidmatan Awam, ACPA);

- Quality Control Circles (Brunei's Kumpulan Kerja Cemerlang, KKC); and

- Review of the Manual Procedure (Brunei's Manual Prosedur Kerja, MPK).

These changes have created an environment in the public service where opportunities are now widely given to lower and middle cadre personnel to participate in the decision making process and to contribute ideas for quality improvement and increased productivity. Formerly, the lower and middle levels were limited to routine duties while ideas for improvement in the organisation were left entirely to the top management. All of the initiatives are of a continuous nature towards improving the overall performance of the public sector.

The Public Service Department (PSD) of Brunei Darussalam plays a central role in the reform programme. The PSD is a central government agency with responsibility for the human resource of the public service. The PSD's mission is to ensure the optimum utilisation of human resource through effective management, planning and development. As a line department in support of the overall Public Service initiatives, the PSD has undertaken changes in the following areas:

- **Clients Charter (TPOR):** Divisional heads are required to submit monthly reports to the Director General on the performance of functional units in keeping with the TPOR. The outcome of these reports vary and in most cases, where there are delays, action is taken to ensure that in future such delays do not recur.

- **Quality Control Circles (KKC):** The management of the PSD hold weekly meetings to consider KKC activities. For the PSD, KKC has been proven to be able to solve problems and to improve matters relating to human resource management and working procedures.

- **Zero Defect:** As one of the central agencies (besides the Treasury and the Audit Department), the PSD despatches an average of 420 correspondence (letters, memoranda) daily. As a way of ensuring that correspondence is received in order and in proper manner, an ad hoc team was assigned to monitor their accuracy. Although the exercise was time consuming and involved a lot of paper wastage, the department can now assure the quality of its correspondence and has thus reduced future paper wastage.

The government recently launched the Public Service of the 21st Century programme which gives direction and focus for the public service in the twenty-first century. The programme aims to create a high quality and excellent public service, one that is efficient, responsive, innovative, credible and accountable. The following challenges have been identified:

- **Demands and effects of globalisation:** The opportunities and challenges posed by globalisation demand that the public sector enhance its capacity in order for the nation to be competitive and have a leading edge.

- **Sustainability and competitiveness:** Brunei Darussalam needs to diversify its economy away from over dependence on oil and gas. The public sector should create an enabling business environment that would attract more investment in order to sustain the living standard of the people now and in the future.

- **Increased expectations:** The public service should be ready to respond to a public that is increasingly vocal, demanding of higher standards of service, and an economy that is increasingly outward oriented.

Besides the traditional role of the public service as a protector of peace and security, enforcer of law and order, controller and service provider, the public service of the twenty-first century should assume the role of:

- **Facilitator:** It should continuously improve itself and enhance the quality of its services.

- **Promoter, developer, innovator and an agent of change:** To assume this role, the public service should be knowledgeable, skilled, creative and innovative in formulating and implementing plans systematically and strategically.

- **Thinker:** As a government agent, the public service should provide critical input for decision making.

Strategies to achieve the goals of the Public Service of the 21st Century include:

- inculcating the public service ethics;

- reviewing the public service to make it more relevant;

- aligning laws and regulations to meet the requirements of the twenty-first century;

- Quality Control Circle as a management culture;

- Clients' Charter;

- Human resource development for public servants;

- Public Service Awards.

INDIA

Country Profile

Location: The Republic of India is located in southern Asia and is bordered by Bangladesh, Bhutan, Myanmar, China, Nepal and Pakistan.

Capital: New Delhi

Area: 3,287,263 sq km

Population: India has a population of over a billion people, 73 per cent of whom live in the rural areas. India is the world's second largest country in terms of population.

Language: The main official languages are Hindi (spoken by 30 per cent of the population), and English (as laid down in the Constitution and Official Languages Act of 1963), but there are also 17 official regional languages.

Government: India became independent in August 1947. It is a federal republic with a bicameral parliamentary democracy.

Economy: India's economic policy has traditionally focused on poverty reduction. From the 1950s to the 1980s, there was a drive towards large-scale industrialisation through government investment in public sector enterprises, notably in heavy industry, aimed at providing employment and increasing self-reliance, with emphasis on import substitution. The outcome is that India is now one of the world's largest industrial economies, with labour-intensive systems. However, few improvements have reached the rural areas where 70 per cent of the population live and depend on agriculture.

Quality and Productivity Concerns in the Public Sector

The state continues to focus attention on its basic responsibilities such as the provision of public goods (roads, courts, regulatory systems), primary education, public health (water, sewage and sanitation), population control and arresting the degradation of common resources (water and forests). However, the carrying out of these responsibilities has been affected by rising fiscal deficits and the expansion of the role of the state.

In addition, there is a continuing need to develop requisite physical infrastructures in the public sector. Similarly, regulatory structures have to be put in place to ensure delivery of quality services and maintenance of standards. The financial sector, for example, requires regulation focusing on transparency, reduction of systemic risk and accountability of the managers. The social sector requires regulation to ensure that information on quality of service is made available to the public. Institutions of governance require dramatic improvement in productivity. Local self government has to be strengthened and given additional roles. The state needs to decentralise powers and functions to the local level so as to improve targeting and productivity of expenditure.

Public sector banks present a further illustration of the prevailing challenges in India. The public sector banks of the country are characterised by high operational cost and low business per employee. One of the main reasons attributed for their poor performance as compared to the private sector banks is the high level of staffing. In 2000, while the establishment expenses as a percentage of total expenses was 3.04 per cent for the private sector bank, it was as high as 20.13 per cent for the public sector banks. Similarly business per employee for the private sector banks was Rs88.5 million while for the public sector banks it was as low as Rs8.9 million.

Public Sector Reform Issues

A number of recommendations aimed at improving the productivity, efficiency and profitability of the public banking system on the one hand and providing it with greater operational flexibility and functional autonomy in decision making on the other, have been made. The implementation of these recom-mendations, which can conveniently be called the second generation of reforms in the banking sector in India, can be classified into three interrelated issues:

♦ actions that need to be taken to strengthen the foundation of the banking sector;

♦ streamlining procedures, upgrading technology and human resource development;

♦ structural changes in the system.

These are designed to cover aspects of banking policy, institutional, supervisory and legislative dimensions. In the area of staff reduction, the Government of India has solicited the views of all the chairmen of public sector banks regarding the feasibility of introducing a Voluntary Retirement Scheme for the bank employees. In the coming years, the implementation of this decision will pose a major challenge for the banking sector as this is likely to be met with stiff resistance from the employees' unions and some other sectors of the society.

MALAYSIA

Country Profile

Location: Lying in central south-east Asia, above Singapore and south of Thailand, Peninsular Malaysia is separated by about 540km of the South China Sea from the Malaysian states of Sabah and Sarawak, which share the island of Borneo with Indonesia and Brunei Darussalam. Malaysian islands include Labuan, Penang and the Langkawi Islands.

Capital: Kuala Lumpur

Area: 329,758 sq km

Population: 21,018,000 (1997), about 80 per cent of whom live in Peninsular Malaysia.

Language: The national language is Malay. English is widely spoken.

Government: Malaysia was created in 1963 through the merging of Malaya (independent in 1957) and the former British Singapore, both of which formed West Malaysia, and Sabah and Sarawak in north Borneo, which composed East Malaysia. Singapore seceded from the union in 1965. Malaysia is a parliamentary democracy with a federal, constitutional monarchy.

Economy: Malaysia is rich in natural resources and its traditional economic strength lay in commodities. The country is still an important source of tin and rubber and produces more than half the world's palm oil. Over the past two decades, however, the character of the economy changed radically as Malaysia developed into a predominantly manufacturing country focusing on export-oriented electronic and electrical equipment, with services as a rising sector. After a brief recession in the mid-1980s, growth was very strong until 1998, when the collapse of some south-east Asian financial markets caught Malaysia in their fall.

Quality and Productivity Concerns in the Public Sector

In 1991, the government enunciated Vision 2020 which states that 'by the year 2020, Malaysia can be a united nation, with a confident Malaysian society, infused by strong moral and ethical values, living in a society that is democratic, liberal and tolerant, caring, economically just and equitable, progressive and prosperous, and in full possession of an economy that is competitive, dynamic, robust and resilient'. The achievement of Vision 2020 demands the emergence of a modernised public service. This would entail a process of readjusting, reinforcing and refocusing the needs and demands of a more dynamic environment.

Public Sector Reform Issues

At the apex of the reform consideration process is the Panel on Administrative Improvements to the Civil Service (PANEL) which has been instrumental in translating reform ideas into reform programmes in the public sector. A significant product of the deliberations of the PANEL is the issuance of Development Administration Circulars (DACs) which spell out the concept and rationale of a particular reform programme. The DACs have come to be recognised as a distinct form of communication relating to administrative reform as opposed to other circulars.

The launch of the 'Excellent Work Culture Movement' is generally seen as the starting point of a concerted reform programme for the 1990s. The thrust of this movement was to inculcate a culture of excellence in public sector agencies based on the core values of quality, productivity, innovation, integrity, discipline, accountability and professionalism.

The provision of customer-oriented services is the main thrust of administrative reform efforts. To ensure the efficient and effective provision of customer-oriented services, public sector agencies are required to focus on the following programmes:

- Total Quality Management (TQM) as an ongoing programme that covers all quality programmes carried out in the public sector;

- innovation at the work place to reduce operational costs, effect time savings and improve productivity;

- Quality Control Circles (QCC) which is premised on the concept of participatory management, and geared towards greater teamwork and empowerment of employees;

- Client's Charter as a written commitment by public sector agencies to set quality standards; and

- Efficient counter services as a crucial factor in the interface between government and the citizen-customer.

The emphasis on information technology (IT) has led to the expansion of IT applications in various areas such as accounting, finance, project management, inventory control, trade documentation and payment of duties. Information technology has also been used to support education and training as well as research and development. The impact of IT can be seen in terms of the introduction of new work flow processes such as electronic data interchange, the development of more public domain databases, the use of Local Area Networks and Wide Area Networks and the increasing use of e-mail.

The Cabinet Committee on the Integrity of Government Management is a key mechanism for oversight of financial management and accountability in the public sector. In this regard, the Prime Minister's Directive No. 1 of 1998 calls for the establishment of management integrity committees at the federal, state and district levels. One of the principal instruments utilised for monitoring management integrity is the annual Auditor-General's Report. Recent amendments to anti-corruption legislation that provide for stringent punishment for graft and abuse as well as the tightening of the disciplinary rules governing the conduct of public officers seek to strengthen efforts at maintaining accountability and discipline in the public sector.

The Malaysian Public Service is involved in three other reform programmes, namely the implementation of MS ISO 9000, benchmarking, and electronic government and e-public services. ISO 9000 requires agencies to comply with a quality management system that emphasises prevention and not a system that caters for remedial action after defects have occurred. Hence, under MS ISO 9000, agencies must carry out a continuous review of the critical processes and take immediate corrective action. This is to ensure the development of work methods of consistent quality based on the principle of *right the first time and all the time* through documented policies and procedures. The Malaysian Civil Service MS ISO 9000 Certificate is issued to those agencies which meet the requirements of MS ISO 9000 in terms of documentation and compliance to standards after going through the adequacy and compliance auditing processes. Surveillance audit is conducted a year after the agency has been accredited to ensure that the agency continues to comply with MS ISO 9000 standards.

The implementation of benchmarking, effected in 1999, is defined as a systematic and continuous process to identify, learn, adapt and implement best practices, either from units within an organisation or from an external organisation in achieving excellent performance. Under this process, the Implementing Agency, which is the agency in search of a best practice, can select a Benchmarking Partner, which is the entity from which the best practice is to be sourced. The benchmarking initiative can help public sector agencies reinforce the basic thrust of TQM which is based on a quality management process that is customer-focused with continuous improvements that involve all aspects of an organisation.

Electronic Government (EG) and E-Public Services (EPS) – The vision of EG is to drastically improve the performance of public administration through the use of multimedia technology and thereby, provide high quality, low cost administrative services to citizens and businesses. Four important documents have been issued in connection with the implementation of EG. They are:

◆ *Towards a Vision for a New Electronic Government in Malaysia* that outlines the vision and objective as well as the benefits of EG;

- *Electronic Government Information Technology Policy and Standards* that defines a framework for a common infrastructure and standards required for inter-operability;

- *Electronic Government Blueprint for Implementation* that elaborates on the specific implementation of EG in the context of the concept, vision and objectives; and

- *Concept Request for Proposals* for the pilot applications calling for proposals from interested parties.

The five key pilot applications in the first stage of EG are the electronic delivery of driver and vehicle registration, licensing and summons services, utility bill payments and Ministry of Health Online Information; Electronic Government Procurement; Project Monitoring System; Human Resource Management Information System; and Prime Minister's Office – Generic Office Environment.

E-Public Services (EPS) envisions a collaborative and proactive relationship between the public, private and voluntary sectors in providing quality services that will enhance productivity through critical success factors. An action plan outlining the role of the public sector and its partners in implementing EPS has been formulated.

MALDIVES

Country Profile

Location: The Republic of Maldives is an archipelago in the Indian Ocean, some 670km west-south-west of Sri Lanka. Its 1,190 coral islands, 199 of which are inhabited, occur on a double chain of 26 coral atolls.

Capital: Malé

Area: While the land area is only an estimated 298 sq km, the country's total area of land and seas is some 90,000 sq km. The archipelago is 823km long and 130km at its widest.

Population: 273,000 (1997). Of the 199 inhabited islands, 90 percent have populations of less than 1000. About 20 per cent of the nation's population live in Malé.

Language: The national language is Dhivehi. English is widely spoken.

Government: Maldives became independent from the United Kingdom in 1965. The country is a democratic republic.

Economy: Tourism is the largest industry, accounting for 20 per cent of GDP and more than 60 per cent of foreign exchange receipts. Over 90 per cent of government tax revenue comes from import duties and tourism-related taxes. Fishing is the second leading sector.

Quality and Productivity Concerns in the Public Sector

Rapid economic growth and social development, expansion of the private sector, active citizenry, exposure of the country to the international arena have contributed to the development of a new perception of the 'proper' role of government. The perceived role of government is to provide better services leading to improvement in the quality of life, timely delivery of service, customer orientation in the delivery service, greater accountability, greater transparency in decision making, performance evaluation and improved quality of service to levels that are comparable to those of the private sector.

For most of the past decade, Maldives operated a deficit budget, leading to pressures to reduce public expenditures. Consequently, expenditures on salaries were restrained for a number of years and there was a virtual freeze on the creation of public service positions. However, at the same time, the public demanded increased efficiency from the public service.

The private sector is actively engaged in various activities that were traditionally reserved for the public sector. The competition has created the fear of losing some of the best qualified and experienced personnel to the higher paid private sector jobs.

With the rapid integration of the Maldives into the world's changing political, economic and social environment, the country is required to keep abreast, at least with regional levels of performance and productivity. Internationalisation of the public service has also required the country to adopt and adhere to a wide rage of international standards and conventions on various aspects. These cannot be achieved without improved public sector performance and increased public sector productivity. Other areas of quality and productivity concerns include:

- ◆ diseconomies of scale in the delivery of social services as the small human population of the country is fragmented and spread over 200 islands;

- ◆ scarcity of resources to meet growing needs;

- ◆ shortage of human resources;

- ◆ inadequate transparency in promotions;

- ◆ low wages making it necessary for those in the public service to take up a second job;

- ◆ inadequate delegation of power, centralised decision making.

Public Sector Reform Issues

Over the years, the government has taken initiatives to create efficiency in the operation of government activities and to improve the standard of services rendered to the public. The National Office for Personnel and Administrative Reform (NOPAR) was created to bring about reforms needed in the overall management of government offices, and to strengthen employment activities, training of personnel, restructuring of organisations and to improve work procedures of government offices. NOPAR, with the assistance of foreign managing consultants, has undertaken a number of important initiatives, some of which are:

- the introduction of public service grading of jobs and a classification system (formulating standard and qualification requirements for the public sector, setting employment standards, writing job descriptions, under-taking job analysis, job evaluation);

- the introduction of professional, technical and long service allowances to government employees;

- publication of manuals documenting rules and regulations was regarded as important to set the minimum required standard of the public service. Such publications include: 'Rules on Spending Government Funds and Hanging Government Assets' 1991; 'Employment Regulation of the Republic of Maldives' 1994; 'Rules and Regulation for the Conduct of Employee Affairs' 1994; and *Handbook on Public Service Performance Appraisal.*

Towards fulfilling the objectives of Vision 2020 for the Maldives, the President established the Public Service Division in October 1999. The aim of the Public Service Division is to determine ways to expedite services provided by the government to the public, to promote best practices and create a culture for continuous improvement. Also in 1999, an eight-member Advisory Committee was appointed to advise the Public Service Division on reforming and modernising the public service in line with the objectives stated in Vision 2020. The specific objectives of the Public Service Division are:

- assist government offices to further improve the procedure of rendering services to the public;

- shape the structure and work procedures as well as moulding the rules and regulations to achieve the established objectives of the government offices;

- hasten the services rendered by the government and expediting the management of government officers by encouraging the use of information technology constructively and efficiently;

- creating awareness among the staff about their role in the public service and increasing the capability of the employees by encouraging and facilitating the provision of necessary training;

- strengthening the opportunities for effective job opportunities, salaries, benefits for government employees and improving the mechanism for maintaining the (office) records of the staff.

In order to give new impetus to the reform activities, the Public Service Division is working on developing selected projects that need urgent attention and improvement. Among them are:

- conducting a series of short seminars for public officials;

- development of a long-term Strategic Plan for Public Sector reform in the Maldives for the next 20 years;

- establishment of an integrated Management Information System;

- evolving customer service and development of one-stop service centres;

- strengthening the human resource functions within government ministries;

- training and development of public sector personnel in managerial, supervisory and operating skills;

- dissemination of information widely by issuing a Public Service Journal, especially focusing on best management practices and research on management;

- establishment of an integrated and incentive oriented performance management systems.

SINGAPORE

Country Profile

Location: The Republic of Singapore is situated in south-east Asia and is separated from Peninsular Malaysia by the Johor Straits. A number of smaller islands are included within its boundaries.

Capital: Singapore

Area: Land area 647.5 sq km including 63 small islands.

Population: 3,439,000 (1997). The population is predominantly Chinese (77 per cent in 1996), with Malays (14 per cent), Indians (7 per cent) and small minorities (1 per cent) Europeans and Eurasians.

Language: Malay, Chinese (Mandarin), Indian (Tamil) and English are all official languages. Malay is the national language, while English is the language of administration and the primary language of instruction in schools.

Government: In 1963, Singapore became a state within Malaysia with internal security, police, customs, defence and foreign affairs under the central federal government. On 9 August 1965, Singapore left Malaysia to become an independent country. It is a republic with an elective, non-executive presidency.

Economy: Singapore originally built its prosperity as an entrepôt base and transhipment centre, and as an importer of its neighbours' raw materials for processing. By the time of independence in 1965, there was a basic electrical assembly industry and some oil refining. During the 1960s, these two sectors took off rapidly, and Singapore swiftly became a world player in the electronics industry. Pharmaceuticals subsequently developed, financial services became a valuable sector and tourism stimulated the economy generally. Singapore imports most of its food and water.

Public Sector Reform Issues

The Singapore public sector needs to be responsive to two major developments: a public that demands increasingly higher standards of service, and an economy that is increasingly outward-oriented. The public sector needs the imagination, pragmatism and flexibility to adapt to new requirements. Many public officials tend to see their job principally as that of observing rules and following precedents. The qualities of consistency and continuity, perceived as the virtues of the public service, can prove to be limitations unless the qualities of flexibility and enterprise are grafted on them.

To prepare public officers for change and for the challenges of the twenty-first century, the Singapore Public Service launched a programme known as Public Service for the 21st Century (PS21) in 1995. PS21 is about inculcating in every public servant a positive attitude towards change and making every public servant an activist for change. The programme focuses on:

♦ **Attitudes:** The essence of this is embodied in the following: 'To be the best, to do the best; to be an active agent for change and continuous improvement; to be a team player where the result of group effort exceeds the sum of the individual efforts.'

♦ **Shared values:** 'We serve the public with courtesy, efficiency and integrity; we are members of a forward-looking, innovative and resource-ful organisation; we care for our staff, value their contributions, and seek to develop them to their fullest potential.'

- **Counter Allowance Scheme:** This was introduced in 1995 to encourage and recognise quality counter service. The intention is to encourage staff serving at counters to be courteous, helpful and efficient when serving the public. A *Service of Excellence Helplist* shows the specific standards of behaviour that supervisors expect of counter staff. The public is also encouraged to give feedback using Service Feedback forms. Assessments of performance are based on inputs from supervisors and feedback forms completed by customers. Outstanding counter staff are rewarded with quarterly bonuses. In 1996, the monthly counter allowance was extended to officers who provide services over the telephone.

- **Work Improvement Teams (WITS):** Under PS21, the concept of WITS has been revamped and all employees are expected to participate in WITS activities in one way or another. The philosophy behind WITS is that an employee should take an interest in their work and make a contribution to their organisation, and should be helped to do so. To enable employees understand this philosophy and to learn WITS tools and techniques, the Civil Service College (Institute of Public Administration and Management) provides training courses. A public sector-wide WITS Convention is held annually to recognise outstanding ministries, departments, teams, facilitators, leaders and members for their contributions to the WITS movement.

- **Staff Suggestions Scheme:** This provides a channel aimed at encouraging every employee, either as individuals or teams/groups to suggest ideas which may be helpful in solving or avoiding problems or improving work processes or the work of the environment. The scheme aims to get the employee used to looking for improvements.

- **Service Improvement Unit (SIU):** The SIU was formed in 1991 as an agency with the authority to monitor, audit, and assess the quality of service provided by government departments and statutory boards, and recommend measures for improvement. The SIU consists of a group of civil servants under the supervision of a political committee of parliament and community leaders. The SIU also provides a mechanism for customers to register their complaints or field their suggestions, and obtain redress (where appropriate) with regard to service provided by government agencies. It looks into every complaint or suggestion brought by the public and ensures that the relevant agency replies to the customer, and makes the necessary change where this is meaningful.

- **Corporate Statement:** A Corporate Statement which sets out the broad performance standards of the civil service was commissioned in 1995. The statement is displayed prominently in all ministries to serve as a reminder both to civil servants and to all their clients of the ideals of the civil service. It reminds the civil service leadership of its mission, and provides them with a set of basic values and points of reference with which to rally the civil service towards meeting the challenges of the future.

◆ **E-Government:** In line with developing a knowledge-based economy, Singapore's electronic- government (e-government) now includes an e-Citizen Centre website. This is a one-stop centre which offers many services based on what a Singaporean citizen might need at different stages of their life. These include birth and death registrations, marriage, family, health, education and business services. There are essentially three arms to the concept of Singapore's e-government. The first is 'government to government' which enables all government departments to be connected and to communicate with each other; the second is 'government to business' which makes government machinery more accessible to businesses; and the third is 'government to citizen' which provides integrated 'customer centric' services in all the areas where people interact with government agencies and departments. Electronic service delivery is cheaper than traditional modes of service delivery, and provides a much higher level of convenience as customers are able to access such services at any time and from anywhere.

SRI LANKA

Country Profile

Location: The Democratic Socialist Republic of Sri Lanka is an island situated in the Indian Ocean, separated from south-east India by the Palk Strait.

Capital: Colombo

Area: 65,610 sq km

Population: The country's population is estimated at 18 million (1997). The largest ethnic group are the Sinhalese (74 per cent), followed by the Sri Lankan Tamils (12 per cent), Indian Tamils (5 per cent), Moors, that is Muslims (7 per cent), minorities of Malays and Burghers (of Dutch or partly Dutch descent) and a small number of Veddhas, descended from the earliest inhabitants.

Language: The official languages are Sinhala and Tamil. English is used in commerce and government and is widely spoken.

Government: Sri Lanka (then Ceylon) became fully independent in 1948. The country assumed the status of a Democratic Socialist Republic and changed its name to Sri Lanka under a new constitution adopted in 1972. The government provides free and compulsory education, widespread health coverage, optional population control measures free of charge and extensive programmes in poverty alleviation.

Economy: While agriculture is central to Sri Lanka's economy, manufacturing and services are of increasing importance, with exports of textiles and clothing now well ahead of the traditional agricultural exports as foreign exchange earners. A banking and financial services sector is also developing. Since 1989, the former policies of nationalisation have been superseded by wide-scale liberalisation, which has led to extensive privatisation of the formerly largely centralised economy.

Public Sector Reform Issues

In the mid-twentieth century, Sri Lanka had a public administration system which was one of the best in the developing countries and attracted some of the most talented personnel. The personnel system was managed by individual cadre committees or boards which recruited, promoted and transferred personnel in exclusive occupational cadres across the public service.

In subsequent years, although the size of the public service and the complexity of its work has increased, and despite several attempts to introduce a more development-oriented administration, the public administration system has remained largely unchanged. By the end of the twentieth century, Sri Lanka's public sector with 57 public sector workers per 1000 population, was oversized in comparison with other countries in the region. This has contributed to a budget deficit of around eight per cent of the GDP. Many of the tasks performed by the public sector in Sri Lanka could, in the context of a liberalised economy, be competently performed through private/NGO agencies. Despite recommendations made by the 1986 Administrative Reforms Committee, the number of cadres have continued to grow, together with ministries, ministers, deputy ministers and personnel. Retrenchment programmes with separation packages were offered in 1990/91 but resulted in those with scarce skills leaving.

Extensive recruitment at lower levels of the public service, given budget constraints, has kept the remuneration of professionals in the service abnormally low. The salary compression ratio is 1:6 compared to 1:10 in the rest of South Asia. The public service now fails to attract sufficient numbers of the best graduates.

The role of the government and the tasks it needs to perform within a market economy and the changing development context (which favours devolution) has yet to be clearly delineated in Sri Lanka. The change of role from being a major provider of goods and services to that of facilitator of economic activity and policy manager has been especially difficult to implement for the following reasons:

- the public service lacks necessary skills as well as appropriate skills training programmes;

- administrative solutions are still preferred for the economic and social issues that public policy should address;

- although an amendment to the Sri Lanka constitution in 1987 divested a lot of power from the central to the provincial level, there is the tendency to continue to perform tasks through centralised structures; thus endeavouring to retain control and management in the ministries at the centre;

- the practices that obtained in the past when there was greater uniformity in job content and a more limited tasks profile in different posts, continue to be followed. This has resulted in inadequate specialisation, frequent transfers from job to job, little commitment to the organisation in which the staff serves, difficulty in enforcing accountability and inability to plan and implement meaningful strategies for task-specific career development.

The first attempt to measure quality and productivity through performance appraisal was introduced only as recently as 1997 and is still being pursued. The latest strategy in public sector reform comprises a three-pronged thrust :

- improving the forward planning, budget and expenditure management process and instituting a resilient personnel management system to ensure that there will be a pool of competent people available to manage the planning and accounting systems across the public service. This programme involves the institutional modernisation of the Ministry of Finance and Planning and the reform of the public financial management and information system across all ministries.

- institutional strengthening of the Sri Lanka Institute of Development Administration to develop into a centre of excellence for public service research, training, advice and consultancy. This will transform it from an institution providing miscellaneous training to the public service to a key player in the public service reform process. Training for a senior management group in the public service was started in 1999 by the institution.

- setting up a Public Service Reform Committee to develop a consistent vision of overall reform, develop coherent strategies to address the major issues and work out an implementation plan with clearly sequenced actions.

CARIBBEAN

THE BAHAMAS

Country Profile

Location: The 'Commonwealth of The Bahamas is a coral archipelago of around 700 islands and over 2,000 rocks and cays in the West Atlantic, south east of the coast of Florida in the United States of America, and north east of Cuba. About 30 islands are inhabited.

Capital: Nassau

Area: 13,939 sq km.

Population: 288,000 (1997), 87 per cent of whom live in the urban areas. Bahamians are largely of African (85 per cent), Afro-European and European origin.

Language: English

Government: The Bahamas became independent from the United Kingdom in 1973. The country is a parliamentary democracy and constitutional monarchy recognising HM Queen Elizabeth II as head of state. She is represented by a Governor-General chosen on the advice of the Cabinet.

Economy: The Bahamas is one of the wealthiest countries in the Caribbean region and one of the world's principal financial centres. The economy is heavily dependent on tourism and offshore banking. Tourism alone accounts for more than 60 per cent of GDP and directly or indirectly employs 40 per cent of the archipelago's labour force. Despite these affluent sectors, the country, which needs to import most of its foodstuff and other products, is vulnerable to global swings, and experienced a recession during the period 1988-1994. This was mainly due to a recession in the United States leading to a fall in the number of American tourists. From the early 1990s, the government undertook an economic reform programme which emphasised diversification of the economy, among others.

Quality and Productivity Concerns in the Public Sector

The public service is the largest employer with over 18,000 employees. The country's strategic geographical location close to North America, makes it susceptible to the direct impact of globalisation. It is, therefore, important that the public sector is able to play the critical role needed to sustain the growth and development of the country. Notable areas of concern in the public service are:

◆ developing a public service culture where there is a high level of shared commitment and quest for excellence;

- reorganising and restructuring (including the devolution and decentralisation of) the components comprising the public service to ensure a more effective system providing a higher standard of service;

- developing a national training policy, manpower training plan, and training facilities that will augment institutional strengthening and human resources capacity building;

- establishing policies, procedures and guidelines that are mutually beneficial to all stakeholders, and ensuring greater transparency and accountability;

- promoting a higher degree of inter-sectoral collaboration and consultation with all public service trade unions and public service representatives;

- employing the use of technology to develop effective management information systems.

Following rising crime levels, mounting public concern and a perception of poor police performance, the government contracted a group of consultants to conduct a strategic review of the Police Force. Their findings and recommendations were documented in a report submitted in 1999. Major areas that should be addressed were highlighted:

- enhance the ability of the police service to manage itself and its staff effectively;

- recognise a number of features which are particular to policing and call for particular qualities and skills of its officers;

- recognise the importance of front line operational duties;

- favour more flexible management structures and enhance spans of management control;

- encourage lateral as well as vertical career development;

- ensure the right level of basic pay is available to recruit and retain good quality officers;

- reflect individual responsibilities, and enhance motivation through an effective and responsible reward system;

- provide reward structures which reward good performance and penalise bad performance;

- ensure that there is greater openness both within the police service and in its dealings with community.

Public Sector Reform Issues

Bahamas Public Service has witnessed the streamlining and re-grouping of similar and related services, and public entities which can be better managed autonomously are being devolved or privatised. Organisation structures are flatter, thereby allowing more decentralisation, devolution of authority, decision making at site based levels, and ensuring greater accountability.

In the area of human resource management and development, existing performance appraisal and assessment/evaluation systems have been improved and new systems created where there were none. There are ongoing aggressive initiatives to identify and train leaders and managers who are proactive, decision makers and change agents. There are service-wide training initiatives to upgrade the current skills of all levels of public officers, commensurate with stated goals and objectives. Wages and salaries are also being reviewed in line with the levels of responsibilities and job functions.

With regard to the Royal Bahamas Police Force, key changes have included the following:

- **Divisional Detectives Units:** In response to the high level of crime in various communities, a decision was made to devolve the Criminal Investigation Department to the Divisional Stations with effect from June 2000. This policy, which does not diminish the role of the Criminal Investigation Department, brings the investigators to the communities and therefore, provides a more effective response to major crime in Divisional areas. It enhances ownership of local crime by Divisional Commanders and offers increased accessibility to Criminal Investigators by persons in the local community.

- **Human resource development:** The government has made a commitment to focus on investing in human resources to ensure that their welfare is given priority and that they are equipped to perform their tasks. Areas of consideration include improved working conditions; advising officers on career development and putting in place a system to facilitate this; sickness and other benefits; improved pension scheme; and improved salaries/promotion scheme aimed at rewarding excellent service, retaining and attracting the 'best and brightest minds' to the Police Force.

- **Police College:** Significant changes are being made at the Police College with the introduction of new methods of training. The aim is to produce a well-trained cadre of officers who will be better able to discharge their duties. It is also expected to reduce the number of lawsuits brought against officers and the organisation for false arrest, unjustifiable or excessive use of force, among others.

BARBADOS

Country Profile

Location: Barbados, the most easterly of the Caribbean islands lies south of St Lucia, east of St Vincent and north of Trinidad.

Capital: Bridgetown

Area: 431 sq km

Population: 262,000 (1997), 48 per cent of whom live in the urban areas. The population comprises 90 per cent of African descent, four per cent of European descent and the remaining six per cent of Asian or mixed descent.

Language: English is the official and first language.

Government: Barbados became an independent sovereign state on 30 November 1966. The country is a parliamentary democracy and constitutional monarchy, recognising the Queen of England as head of state. She is represented by the Governor General.

Economy: Historically, the Barbadian economy was dependent on sugarcane cultivation and related activities, but production in recent years has diversified into manufacturing and tourism. In the 1990s, tourism and manufacturing surpassed the sugar industry in economic importance. The government continues its efforts to reduce high unemployment rate, encourage direct foreign investment, and privatise remaining state-owned enterprises.

Quality and Productivity Concerns in the Public Sector

The traditional role of government was that of maintaining law and order and providing certain minimal social services. The transformation of the role of government since independence in 1966 has been accompanied by a significant growth in staff numbers and agencies which make up the public service. Existing agencies have been expanded and new ones established to implement government's expanded programme of social and economic development.

However, the expansion of the role of government has not been matched with the appropriate tools to manage change in the public service. Past traditions and a commitment to doing things the old way characterise the everyday operations of the public sector. Routine procedures, slow pace, inappropriate precedents are among factors which inhibit effective work output and quality of service.

The structure of the Barbados public sector lends itself to centralisation of authority and responsibility for nearly every function. This has resulted in top level decision making, duplication and overlapping which produce bottlenecks and red tape. There is an overload at the centre, causing long service delays. The disinclination to delegate has become rigid and over-emphasised over time.

Wages and salaries account for a high portion of the government's current expenditure. In order to meet this bill, funds are raised from taxation and domestic borrowing sources. These sources, therefore, demand value for service in terms of the monies paid to public servants.

Public Sector Reform Issues

Previous efforts by the government to improve the public sector include the assignment of a United Nations Advisor in 1971, the establishment of an Organisation and Management Unit in 1974 and a Ministry of the Public Service in 1986. Some changes were achieved, but it was evident that further changes were needed for a major strategic impact on the operations of the public service. In the past decade, the government again embarked on a programme of reform aimed at making the public service respond to the rapidly changing socio-economic, political and technological environment in a non-traditional way. The change goals for the public service focus on people, organisational processes and structures. The government's main proposal in its latest effort is to decentralise authority and responsibility for some functions to lower levels of management. The implementation of such a structure is aimed at facilitating lower level decision making and eliminating areas of duplication and overlapping.

Standards of measurement of performance are imperative to make the public service accountable if government's purpose, direction and goals are to be attained. To this end, a new performance appraisal system to measure the productivity of public officers was introduced on a pilot scheme basis from April 2000.

Scarce economic resources mean that a results-oriented management style rather than consistency in following traditional procedures will change the power relationships of the power brokers in the public sector. The concept of productivity as an important component for the improvement of efficiency in the public service has begun to alter the roles of trade unions, political parties and the bureaucracy. This process of change is expected to continue as greater emphasis is placed on quality outputs and customer satisfaction.

BELIZE

Country Profile

Location: Belize is bordered in the north by the Republic of Mexico, in the south and west by the Republic of Guatemala and to the east by the Caribbean Sea.

Capital: Belmopan

Area: 22,965 sq km

Population: The country has a multi-ethnic population of approximately 250,000.

Language: English is the official language; Spanish is widely spoken.

Economy: Belize's economy is predominantly agricultural with heavy dependence on sugar export. Efforts have been made to diversify into other export products, notably bananas, citrus concentrates and seafood. Forestry has been revitalised and tourism expanded.

Government: Belize became independent in 1981 after having attained self-government in 1961. The government functions as a parliamentary democracy based on the Westminster system. Under its constitution, members of the House of Representatives are elected by the people while members of the Senate are appointed by the Governor General on the advice of the Prime Minister (who is head of the Cabinet), the Leader of the Opposition, and the Governor General in his own deliberate judgement.

Public Sector Reform Issues

Over the years, there have been a series of reviews of the Belize Public Service. Between the 1970s and 1980s, approaches to public service reforms were motivated primarily by structural adjustment programmes of the International Monetary Fund (IMF) and the World Bank. The over-riding international strategy was two-pronged: reduction in public expenditure, mainly in the social sectors, accompanied by wage restraints and retrenchment of government employees; and privatisation and divestment of state owned enterprise to generate capital for debt repayment to the international financial institutions.

Historically, there have been no less than 13 attempts towards the revision and diagnosis of the Belize public service. Generally, these attempts have had as a main objective, the need to satisfy the demand by the Belizean people for public service delivery that is timely, efficient and proficient. Furthermore, the government recognises the need for a dynamic public sector that is able to meet the challenges of the information technology age.

In January 2000, the Prime Minister appointed the Public Sector Reform Council with a mandate to advise on and coordinate the implementation of the public sector reform. Following a review of the structure of government and the public sector, previous reform efforts, and the current status of the public service, the Council developed a number of strategies, some of which are highlighted below:

- **Rationalise the roles and functions of ministries:** Such a revision aims to promote:
  - the efficient planning, implementation and evaluation of all programmes and projects;
  - coordinate the essential resource and service departments to focus on the national and grassroots objectives and priorities as determined in each development sector;
  - develop effective linkages in partnership with the private sector and civil society that can pool resources and services, both from national and external sources, to further the objectives and priorities of the development sectors;
  - optimally distribute human and financial resources between the administrative and implementation branches of government.

- **Improve policy development and coordination:** Underlying this is a macro-economic strategy which presents the policies of the Belize government to successfully meet the challenge of stabilising the economy's competitiveness, and setting the stage for sustainable development. Policy units within key ministries (such as the Ministries of Health, Education and Natural Resources) are responsible for policy coordination and development; planning, programming and budgeting; monitoring, evaluation and feedback; staff development through training; analysis and advice in respect of projects to determine whether they fall within the policy framework; and the collection, storage and publication of statistics and information, among others. Furthermore, interministerial as well as special Committees and Commissions drawn from the public and private sectors continue to be used to provide advice to drive forward the government agenda.

- **Improve public sector performance (review of systems):** Under this strategy, procedure manuals and other management guidelines are reviewed, developed and published as necessary from time to time. Administrative procedures are simplified to accelerate and facilitate performance. This is done through the reduction of unnecessary steps and red tapism without losing the basic content, and safeguarding the public interest. Personal and institutional accountability is enforced through the following means:

- developing and strengthening favourable work ethics;
- performance contracts for senior executives;
- comprehensive auditing procedures (including performance and financial audits of ministries);
- recognition of outstanding performance and prompt delivery of awards and incentives; and
- enforcement of the disciplinary code.

◆ **Improve human resource development:** Staff training and development continues to receive top priority. Priority is given to the formulation of a training needs analysis which serves as a guide for training programmes both at the national and sectoral levels.

◆ **Improve application of information technology:** The government has embarked on the following projects aimed at modernising and making the public service more efficient:
- automated management systems for all government agencies;
- a human resource management information system in the ministry responsible for the public service;
- standardised information systems throughout the public service; and
- the establishment of an Information Technology Unit to render operational support as well as enforce policy compliance.

BRITISH VIRGIN ISLANDS

Country Profile

Location: British Virgin Islands is a United Kingdom Overseas Territory situated in the Caribbean, about 80 km east of Puerto Rico, north of the Leeward Islands, and adjacent to the United States Virgin Islands. It is made up of over 40 islands, 16 of which are inhabited.

Capital: Road Town

Area: The territory covers an areas of 153 sq km. The largest of the islands are Tortola (54 sq km), Anegada (39 sq km), Virgin Gorda (21 sq km) and Jost Van Dyke (9 sq km).

Population: The country has a population of approximately 20,000 concentrated on the four largest islands.

Language: The official language is English.

Economy: Tourism and financial services form the mainstay of the economy, supplemented by agriculture and fishing.

Government: The British Virgin Islands is a United Kingdom Overseas Territory with self-government in most internal matters. The Queen of England is represented by an appointed Governor who has certain discretionary powers. Policy decisions are made by the local legislature.

Public Sector Reform Issues

Although various institutions of the public service have been the focus of recent attention, the education sector has arguably attracted a good deal of interest. The mission statement of the Ministry of Education and Culture is to ensure the provision and delivery of high quality services to the people of the British Virgin Islands via recurrent and new capital projects, programmes, policies, finance and the necessary legislation in the respective areas of Education, Culture, Library Services, Museums, Archives, Sports and Recreation. The Ministry of Education and Culture has oversight for three Departments, namely Education and Culture, Library Services, Sports and Recreation. The ministry concerns itself mainly with policies, finance and legislation while the departments concentrate on the management and administration of their respective activities and programmes.

The British Virgin Islands has a long history of providing mass education for its people. Literacy rate stands at 94 per cent (Development Planning Unit – 1990 Census Report) and where certain types of educational opportunities are not available locally, the government sponsors students to attend regional and international institutions of higher learning.

The main areas of quality and productivity concerns in the Ministry of Education and Culture are largely reflective of the concerns experienced in the public sector as a whole.

◆ **Planning:** The 'First Five-Year Development Plan for Education' (1990) emphasised the urgent need for effective planning. The Plan stated: 'Planning is currently a neglected area of expertise within the educated system.' In yet another section, it continued: 'The lack of a plan for education is being felt in the British Virgin Islands as the pace of economic development quickens and manpower shortages become more keenly experienced. Ad hoc measures to improve the quantity and quality of outputs from the school system only serve to focus the need for a comprehensive plan which seeks to avoid unattainable targets and dislocation internal to the educational system.' A decade later, effective planning is still a critically deficient area, with the attitude being one of reaction rather than pro-action to situations. Not only is there a need for effective and efficient planning, but it is equally important that the administrative staff develop the competency to manage these responsibilities.

◆ **Information sharing and communication:** Effective information and communication are the hub of any organisation. Often times, good ideas are shared, but the necessary actions needed to solve or alleviate the problems are slow to be effected. Also, it would appear that the possession of information is personalised, so that when a person with some vital information is absent, that information cannot be obtained. There is, therefore, the need to implement an effective succession plan to ensure continuous smooth operation. There is also the need for the maintenance of a proper Management Information System.

◆ **Curriculum reform:** There is a need to reform the curriculum in order to make education more relevant to the territory's manpower needs, especially in the thriving tourism and financial services sectors. Other areas of concern are the efficient and effective management of resources, budget preparation and staff training.

Against the background of the foregoing, the following reform issues have been embarked on:

◆ a review of the education system to produce a new five-year education plan which would address issues on the infrastructure, curriculum development, management reform, manpower policy, legislation, training and support services;

◆ the construction of a technical/vocational institution to cater for the territory's needed skill areas;

◆ the inclusion of a compulsory second/third language in both primary and secondary schools;

◆ computer classes taught throughout the school system;

◆ the computerisation of the ministry and departments and the networking of the ministry to other OECS Ministries of Education, as well as the provision of intranet and internet services in the ministry and its departments;

◆ improvements in the filing system; and

◆ administrative/staff changes within the ministry.

DOMINICA

Country Profile

Location: The Commonwealth of Dominica is one of the Windward Islands in the Eastern Caribbean, lying between Guadeloupe to the north and Martinique to the south.

Capital: Roseau

Area: 750 sq km

Population: 71,000 (1997). The population is mostly of African and African/European descent, with European, Syrian and Carib minorities.

Language: The official language is English.

Government: Dominica achieved independence as a republic on 3 November 1978. The country is a parliamentary democracy.

Economy: The economy depends mainly on agriculture. Agriculture, primarily bananas, accounts for 21 per cent of GDP and employs 40 per cent of the work force. Despite its sustained rates of growth, Dominica's economy is vulnerable. Its location exposes it to tropical storms and hurricanes, which have caused severe damage to the crops making up the country's economic base. The government has, therefore, introduced measures to diversify the economy. Since the 1980s, it has been working to develop export-oriented small industries, notably garments and electronics assembly. It has also encouraged development of tourism, especially eco-tourism.

Public Sector Reform Issues

The responsibility and authority for public sector matters in Dominica are shared mainly by four offices. At the ministerial level, the minister is responsible for overall policy direction while the Permanent Secretary is responsible for administrative and management issues. At the national level, the Establishment, Personnel and Training Department (EPTD) is responsible for negotiating and co-ordinating terms and conditions of employment, personnel matters and training throughout the service. The authority for appointment and discipline in the service rests with the Public Service Commission. There are a range of factors that influence efficiency and productivity in Dominica's public service, notably:

- the continued use of out-dated laws and regulations to manage and guide the service;

- the timeliness of appropriate actions and interventions which leaves much to be desired;

- the concept and principles of accountability are not always practised and observed;

- there exists a lack of commitment on the part of many public officers.

Locally, regionally and internationally, the state and by extension the public sector is presently seen as a facilitator and regulator in a market economy which is private sector led. Taxpayers and by extension the general public expect and demand value for money. The public has become more sophisticated, educated, better informed and politically aware. They are aware of the characteristics of quality services and are also aware of their legal and constitutional rights.

For several years now, Dominica has been involved in the task of public sector reform. An important strategy has been the development of a customer-oriented focus within the public sector. Elements of such a focus include the establishment of service standards, provision of improved waiting facilities in public buildings, the establishment of mechanisms for more convenient and timely delivery of service, the establishment of a framework to address complaints and provide redress on a timely basis as and where appropriate, the establishment of a system for monitoring and collection of feedback.

Some sub-sectors of Dominica's public service have been specially targeted in the reform programme. These sub-sectors include the Department of Education, Police Service, Community Development Department, as well as the Ministry of Agriculture and the Environment. The reform process in the Division of Agriculture deserves highlighting.

The main areas of concern in this sector were that all the professional staff operated from the head office and generally observed regular working hours; and services (for example extension and veterinary services) were provided from a central base. The results were poor extension services to farmers and regular complaints from them. In addition, the volume of agricultural production and the quality of produce were on the decline. To change this trend, the Division was re-structured and sub-divided into seven districts with a team of agricultural professionals and technicians based in each district. Each team is headed by a professional. These changes aim to provide more efficient and effective services to the farmers, give timely response to their concerns and foster a better relationship between the farmers and technical advisers. All of these are expected to result in improved quality and volume of agricultural produce.

JAMAICA

Country profile

Location: Jamaica, the third largest island in the Caribbean is situated south of Cuba and west of Haiti.

Capital: Kingston

Area: 10,991 sq km

Population: The country has a population of around 2.5 million, approximately one million of whom live in the capital. The population is predominantly of African descent, with European, East Indian and Chinese descended minorities, and some people of mixed descent.

Language: English and English-based Creole.

Government: Jamaica gained full independence in 1962. The country is a parliamentary democracy and a constitutional monarchy with the Queen of England as the titular head of the country represented by a Governor General.

Economy: Historically, the Jamaican economy had an agricultural base, dependent on a few staple export crops, primarily sugar and banana. New economic development began with bauxite mining (after 1952) and the tourism boom in the 1950s and 1960s. In the 1990s, tourism became the major earner of foreign exchange.

Quality and Productivity Concerns in the Public Sector

The 1960s saw the expansion of the state bureaucracy and the advent of new economic interest groups. The 1970s was a period when a host of public enterprises and public sector companies were created consistent with the then government's commitment to the ideology of democratic socialism and a greatly expanded role in the economy. By the mid 1980s, as a result of devaluation of the currency and structural adjustments, it became necessary to reduce the size of government. In January 1992, a Committee of Advisors on Government was set up to study the structure and role of the public service in the new economic context, which is market-based by liberalisation and deregulation. The committee noted that the local perception of the function of government was that of an over-staffed, slow, lumbering bureaucracy characterised by low morale in the exercise of its functions. There was a clear need to restructure and reform all areas of government, to make it leaner, more cost effective, more facilitative and supportive of the development process. The committee further identified the following problems:

- organisational fragmentation (duplication of functions and overlapping jurisdiction/authority, loss of financial accountability, parallel personnel systems – differential salary scales);

- weak policy and decision making mechanisms (distinction between policy making and policy implementation was blurred, decision taking was alien to the system, and few permanent secretaries gave primacy to strategic functions);

- rejection of new managerialism (adherence to job security, lack of urgency in policy implementation, rudimentary approaches to management of capital assets);

- misunderstanding the dynamics of minister and civil servant relations;

- ministers not giving primacy to the performance of strategic management tasks (monitoring of progress, accountability, inter-ministerial collaboration);

- an overgrown and inflexible governmental machinery.

Public Sector Reform Issues

Since the late 1980s, reforms have been undertaken designed to effect the delivery of government's goods and services in a timely and cost-effective manner, focusing on the overall rationalisation of the public sector, the creation of executive agencies; strengthening of procurement procedures and the establishment of a demand-led training programme. In May 1998, the government approved public sector reforms based on:

- foundations of the reforms: Financial Management Information Programme; Human Resource Information System; storage and retrieval of information; improving customer service; widening the concept of accountability of permanent secretaries and heads of departments; improving the system of procurement of goods and services; merging of entities and sharing of corporate services; divesting health services delivery; improving the system of tax administration and regulation; contracting-out of certain services; privatisation of entities; closing down of redundant state entities; and the establishment of service delivery entities or executive agencies;

- the establishment of executive agencies (an organisational approach which has proved successful in the United Kingdom and New Zealand). These executive agencies, headed by a Chief Executive Officer, will be able to recruit staff, terminate staff appointments and appoint accounting officers without approval from the central government as a means to improve efficiency and effectiveness, and the quality of customer service.

In 1995, in pursuance of its policy to encourage private sector investment in the utilities sector, the government created an independent regulator – the Office of Utilities Regulation. The agency was formally launched by the Prime Minister in 1997. The OUR acts as the complaint agency of last resort and, through the Consumer Affairs Department, takes complaints from customers who have exhausted the complaint handling machinery of the utility companies and remain dissatisfied.

As the OUR evaluates the efficiency and quality of service rendered by the utility companies, it must itself demonstrate a high level of efficiency and quality. It was fully appreciated that the costs for supporting the OUR would ultimately reflect in the tariffs paid by users of the utility services and, therefore, every effort should be made to promote a culture concerned about minimising overheads and costs. Perhaps, the decision that has most significantly impacted on the evolving culture of the agency relates to staffing. The adoption of a flat organisational structure, the use of teams to accomplish tasks and the use of technology has enabled the OUR to minimise the numbers of persons on staff. It does mean, however, that the agency has to contract help on those occasions when the work load is at a peak. This approach is considered to be more efficient and also serves the purpose of ensuring that staff are fully occupied. The agency also sets itself a number of quality benchmarks which are summarised below:

◆ written complaints are acknowledged within five business days of receipt and complainants advised as to when investigations will be completed;

◆ case letters (OUR's written requests to the utilities for information) are prepared and dispatched to the utility companies within five days of receipt of the complaint;

◆ investigations are completed and a final response sent to the complainant within 40 business days. In the event that an investigation is likely to extend beyond the 40 days, the complainant is advised prior to the expiration of the period and a new commitment made;

◆ appointments are offered, scheduled and kept;

◆ messages left on the voice mail answering facility are responded to within two business hours.

In order to encourage serious attention to the attainment of these benchmarks, the agency's performance in respect of these is published quarterly.

MONTSERRAT

Country Profile

Location: Montserrat is one of the Leeward Islands in the Eastern Caribbean, lying 43km south west of Antigua and 64km north west of Guadeloupe.

Capital: Plymouth

Area: 102 sq km

Population: 3,500 (mid-1998), rising to 4,500in 1999 as Monteserratians return. Most of the island's population of 12,771 (1996 estimate) left the country following the eruption of the Soufriere Hills volcano that began in the mid-1990s.

Language: English

Government: Montserrat is an internally self-governing United Kingdom Overseas Territory. A Governor administers the dependency with the assistance of executive and legislative councils.

Economy: In the 1980s, the main economic activities were agriculture and tourism with some light engineering. Hurricane Hugo destroyed 90 per cent of infrastructure in September 1989, severely damaging the tourism and agriculture sectors. Since then the main economic activity has been reconstruction which suffered a major set-back when volcanic activity began in 1995.

Public Sector Reform Issues

During the mid 1990s, personal emoluments was assessed at 65 per cent of total recurrent expenditure of Montserrat. It was, therefore, thought that there should be a reduction in staff, which would enable a better mix of staff cost and other services provided by the government. However, before the changes could be effected, the Soufriere Hills volcano became active. The fear of living with an active volcano forced many persons, including many experienced civil servants to leave the island. This immediately led to a natural attrition of staff.

Due to the shortage of trained staff, the efficiency and effectiveness of the public sector was drastically reduced. In a number of cases, the quality of the output of staff fell below the required standard. This was primarily due to the fact that in the face of staff shortage, the public sector was forced to hire staff who did not possess all the requisite skills and abilities to perform their duties. Thus, in addition to an increased workload, the remaining staff have had to undertake the continuous training of 'green' staff. Staff may not readily accept their expanding roles; duties and responsibilities, especially in the case where there is no corresponding increase in pay.

This, therefore, has the potential to create conflict between staff and management.

Montserrat relies heavily on donor agency funding for training. In recent years, it has become more difficult to access these sources of funding. Consequently, the public sector has been unable to provide quality human resource development and training for staff. The lack of adequate training means that some functions are being ignored or are not being performed effectively, efficiently and economically.

Living with an active volcano places additional strain on public service employees. Although people are generally coping with the phenomenon, increased volcanic activity and its accompanying uncertainties, negatively affect the output of staff.

At present, there is an Administration Department with centralised human resource management, development, training and general welfare. There is a move to create a specialist Personnel Department within the Administration Department. Centralised personnel functions will remain within the Personnel Department. However, some of the personnel management functions will be devolved to line managers within the various ministries/departments.

A Resource Allocation Review was conducted in 1997 to examine the appropriate levels of staff required to enable each department to function efficiently and effectively. The recommendations of the review are now being implemented. Some staff positions were made redundant; the duties and responsibilities of some positions were expanded and some positions were created where there was the need for additional functions to be performed.

Prior to the Resource Allocation Review, line managers had no say in the selection of staff. This function was within the sole purview of the Public Service Commission. In recent years, the line manager has become a member of the selection committee that interviews the applicant. This enables the line manager to obtain the services of the applicant with the best mix of requisite knowledge, fundamental qualities and interpersonal skills.

A Job Evaluation Review, requiring the preparation of job descriptions for job evaluation purposes, has been embarked on. Staff in selected positions are interviewed to gain an understanding of their major activities, supervision received, supervisory responsibilities, decisions made, knowledge, etc. It is envisaged that the review will enable the correct placement of staff within the public service, in terms of work load and salary structure.

In addition, most of the public service have been or are in the process of being computerised. In the Treasury Department, for example, plans are underway to move from a line budgeting to a programmed budgeting system. Within the Audit Department, there is a changing focus from purely financial audits to conducting more comprehensive audits that include computer auditing and value for money auditing.

ST LUCIA

Country Profile

Location: St Lucia is one of the Windward Islands groups jutting out from the Eastern Caribbean into the Atlantic. It lies south of Dominica and north of Barbados.

Capital: Castries

Area: 616 sq km

Population: 146,000 (1997). Most of the island's population are of African and European descent.

Language: English, French-based Creole and French.

Government: St Lucia became independent in February 1979. It is a constitutional monarchy with the Queen of England as head of state represented by a Governor General.

Economy: Although St Lucia's national income is relatively high among developing countries, it is disadvantaged by its economic dependence on bananas and by its small size, small population and human resources. It has successfully exploited opportunities in tourism and small-scale industry, making use of trade preferences from the United States and the European Union, and creating a more diverse economy, with better developed manufacturing, than its neighbours.

Quality and Productivity Concerns in the Public Sector

There is general consensus that the administrative machinery of the State must be improved to meet the demands of a rapidly changing domestic and global environment. The calls for increased productivity and sensitivity to the consumers of public goods and services, and the growing concerns for value for money are some of the issues raised by the general public, private sector organisations, labour associations and other interested parties. Public managers themselves have also recognised the need for the public service to undergo the process of self assessment and renewal, if the competencies of public officers are to be effectively utilised to achieve stated targets.

Thus environmental scanning, ongoing research and experimentation, and the creation of a climate of change and innovation infused with decisive and creative leadership and management are essential. The Government White Paper on Public Sector Reform recognises that over the years, a number of activities aimed at improving the capacity of the State's administrative machinery have taken place. However, public sector reform is an ongoing activity. Therefore, there must be a culture of continuous reflection on past activities to ensure that they remain compatible with current and future goals of the state.

Public Sector Reform Issues

The government is concerned about the ability of the state's administrative arm to efficiently and effectively achieve its mandate. Issues of the size of the public service and the expenditure on the state sector have raised concerns over whether value for money is provided to the general public. Increasingly, citizens are demanding greater participation in the affairs of government, as well as quality public goods and services.

The twenty-first century has been characterised as the information age, as increasingly organisations are harnessing, improving and managing in order to secure competitive advantages and be more effective and efficient in delivering quality services. The harnessing of modern trends in information technology and the development and refinement of management information systems, has called into question the existing structure, policies, processes and mode of relationship which exist between the public service and other organisations.

Furthermore, the changing world economic environment and the formulation of trading blocs have witnessed a decline in the sources of, and quota of aids, grants and other funds made available to developing countries. Government, therefore, has to operate with decreases in revenue generated. Consequently, it has to find innovative ways to utilise available resources to facilitate the socio-economic development of its citizens.

The vision of the ongoing reform effort is to develop a more effective and efficient public service capable of delivering quality service at optimal cost; and is imbued with a strong ethical, professional and national development orientation. This reform is aimed at:

♦ the maximisation of returns from scarce resources through relevant training;

♦ the design and establishment of appropriate structures and the introduction of innovative management approaches;

♦ a heightened sense of responsibility with a focus on accountability and productivity; enhanced self-esteem, job satisfaction and better customer services;

♦ improved effectiveness of revenue collection agencies;

♦ co-ordination and integration of ongoing actions into a rational plan;

♦ a change in the work culture of the public service;

♦ a focus on management, leadership and technology;

♦ help eliminate wastage in all its various forms.

Three important aspects of this reform programme are further outlined below.

♦ **Strategic planning:** The adoption of a strategic planning approach is a necessary prerequisite for a modern public service. This requires that all ministries and departments prepare a clear mission supported by functional objectives, which must be monitored to ensure that the expected results are achieved. The process of strategic planning is facilitated through the establishment of a planning team within each ministry/department. This team, which is multi-disciplinary in its approach and headed by the Deputy Permanent Secretary or other senior personnel, has the following mandate:

- to develop and review the mission and core activities of the ministry/department;
- determine and prioritise activities to be undertaken pursuant to the mission of the ministries/departments;
- develop the strategies for the attainment of organisational objectives;
- identify the resources, human, physical, financial and material that are required;
- establish time frames for the accomplishment of each activity;
- establish the mechanism for periodical review of the achievement of the plan.

♦ **Development of new performance evaluation processes and procedures:** The development of this initiative is being done through the establishment of a committee comprising representatives of the unions representing civil servants, the Permanent Secretary of the Ministry of the Public Service and the Permanent Secretary of any Ministry under consideration. The purpose of this Committee is to review the current process and to make recommendations on the introduction of new processes and procedures. The new public service culture would require that the performance of all employees be periodically assessed. This would include Permanent Secretaries and Heads of Department are traditionally not evaluated.

♦ **Setting standards and quality control:** Strategies needed to achieve this reform goal are:

- a statement as to what each ministry/department aims to achieve and with what resources;
- the expected quality of the services provided, for example waiting time, accuracy of information;
- documentation of the various processes and activities of each ministry and the communication of such to both the internal and external clients of each ministry;
- the identification of a suitable officer or officers to ensure that those standards are adhered to;

- control mechanism for ensuring the adherence to standards. Such control mechanisms would include both reward and sanctions for poor performance;
- the commitment of management personnel and the political directorate to quality and the implementation of quality programmes.

TRINIDAD AND TOBAGO

Country Profile

Location: The country, the most southerly of the West Indian island states, situated 11.2km off the Venezuelan coast, consists of two islands, Trinidad and Tobago.

Capital: Port of Spain

Area: 5,128 sq km (Trinidad 4,828 sq km and Tobago 300 sq km).

Population: 1,307,000 (1997). The population is about 40 per cent African and 41 per cent Indian descent, with smaller numbers of people of European, Latin American and Chinese descent.

Language: English is the official and national language.

Government: The country got its independence from the United Kingdom on 31 August 1962. It is a parliamentary democracy.

Economy: Trinidad and Tobago has a sophisticated economy embracing mineral extraction, agriculture, industry, tourism and services, but which is underpinned by a single commodity, oil, which was discovered in 18666. The country has earned a reputation as an excellent investment site for international businesses. Successful economic reforms were implemented in 1995, and foreign investment and trade are flourishing. Persistently high unemployment remains one of the chief challenges of the government. The petrochemical sector has spurred growth in other related sectors, reinforcing the government's commitment to economic diversification.

Quality and Productivity Concerns in the Public Sector

The following statements represent some of the major issues associated with public sector reform initiatives:

♦ the public service is over-staffed and over-sized;

♦ the public service is lazy, unproductive and inefficient;

- public officers are inadequately compensated;

- the public service is overly bureaucratic and replete with bottlenecks;

- the public service employees are uncaring and discourteous, and have no regard for timeliness and punctuality

- the public service is supportive of workers who are non-performers;

- the public service is a museum of antiquated equipment and offices;

- the public service is poorly managed;

- the public service is costs the country too much;

- there are too many people doing the same thing in the public service;

- the public service cannot be trusted;

- public officers are not held accountable.

In the mid-1990s, the government decentralised the management of public health facilities to four Regional Health Authorities (RHAs). The government's intention was to make adequate health care readily available to all sections of the population, regardless of income or proximity to a major urban hospital. However, the RHAs' responsibilities to deliver health have been compromised because of a shortage of nurses and doctors in certain specialities.

Although the RHA Act vested all public health care facilities (properties) along with the other assets to the RHAs, the staff assigned to public health care facilities were given the options of secondment to an RHA, remaining in the public service (reporting to the Ministry of Health) or transferring to an RHA. As at 2001, 95 per cent of the employees are employed in the public service. The RHAs have not been able to attract the public servants across to their employ for several reasons. Some of these are the perception that there is no job security in the RHAs (as opposed to the public service), and that there is a lack of clearly defined Human Resource Policies and Procedures with regards to terms and conditions of employment.

Public Sector Reform Issues

The vision of the public service of Trinidad and Tobago is that of 'a re-created, continuously improving service organisation, conducting its affairs purposefully and with the highest levels of professionalism and integrity'. Reform programmes towards fulfilling this vision and creating a new public administration are underpinned by declarations of significant principles and values, namely that:

- there must be clarity of purpose and function for every public service entity;

- there must be clear distinction between policy direction and operational activities;

- public service activities must be separated according to services that are of commercial value and those that are core and primarily about service delivery;

- deregulation is to be pursued actively and meaningfully where necessary;

- there is to be a balanced focus on outputs, outcomes and highest quality remits vis-à-vis focus on inputs/processes;

- persons in charge must manage their resources with objectives and success indicators clearly identified;

- responsibility and accountability are to be devolved to the most appropriate levels where decisions and actions are taken;

- there is to be greater balance in the provision of incentives and in the enforcement of sanctions;

- full costs are to be determined for all services provided;

- employment reforms are to ensure high standards in recruitment and selection and for excellent performance;

- issues of transparency and accountability are serious imperatives and priorities;

- the context and impact of reform activities, in particular, will always be considered thoroughly;

- the integrity and spirit of the constitution are to be preserved;

- economic efficiency is to be one of the hallmarks of the new public administration;

- attention to the customer means ensuring competitiveness that exceeds expectations of service delivery of the highest quality.

The government has also initiated a Health Sector Reform programme (HSRP) designed to increase the efficiency and availability of health care in the country. The Ministry of Health had direct control over all of the public health facilities in the country and oversaw all aspects of their operations. Legislative changes were made via the Regional Health Authorities Act (1994) (RHA Act) which effectively decentralised the management of public health facilities to four Regional Health Authorities.

According to the RHA Act, the powers and functions of a Regional Health authority include:

♦ the provision of efficient health care delivery systems, including the facilitation of new health care systems;

♦ collaboration and advice on public health matters;

♦ the management and operation of all property within its boundaries;

♦ collaboration with the University of the West Indies and any other recognised training institution involved in the education and training of health care professionals.

EUROPE

CYPRUS

Country Profile

Location: Cyprus is an island located in the East Mediterranean basin, south of Turkey, west of Syria, north of Egypt and east of Rhodes.

Capital: Nicosia

Area: 9,251 sq km

Population: 861,000 (1997), comprising Greek Cypriots (approximately 80 per cent), Turkish Cypriots, and small populations of Armenians, Maronites and other minorities.

Language: The official languages are Greek and Turkish. English is widely spoken.

Government: Cyprus has a presidential democracy. The 1960 constitution has provisions to ensure a balance of power between the Greek and Turkish communities. In 1996, a system of proportional representation was introduced. The executive comprised a Greek President, a Turkish Vice President and a Council of Ministers (cabinet) with seven Greek and three Turkish members. The ratio of Greek to Turk in the army must be 6:4, and 7:3 in the police, judiciary and civil service.

Economy: The county is a well known regional holiday resort and a services centre (mainly banking and shipping). During the last decade, the Cyprus economy has intensified links with the European Union, its largest trading partner. In 1990, the government submitted an application to become a full member of the European Union. Substantive accession negotiations between Cyprus and the European Union began in 1998.

Public Sector Reform Issues

Problem areas in the public sector in Cyprus relate mainly to:

- increased overall cost and burden to the economy;

- low productivity and hence decreasing efficiency and effectiveness;

- increasing demands for additional and more complex services.

It was, therefore, obvious that concerted efforts were necessary to reform the public sector to enable it meet the present demands and rise to the future challenges of European integration. With the above in mind, the Cyprus government designed a public sector reform programme which came into effect at the beginning of 1996 and includes three categories of measures aimed at:

- reducing the size of the public service and the rate of increase in the cost of the salaries of civil servants;

- improving the organisational structure, procedures and methods of management and operation of the public service in order to increase its productivity, efficiency and effectiveness; and

- creating the positive culture and attitudes necessary to facilitate the introduction of the required changes in the public service so as to transform it into an organisation able to respond to a greater extent to the demands of the state and the desires of the public.

Public sector reform continues to be one of the main targets of government policy as defined in the Strategic Development Plan covering the period 1999-2003. The Plan for the Reform of the Public Service was drawn up by a team of officers from the Ministry of Finance, the Planning Bureau and the Public Administration and Personnel Services (PAPS) who worked under the direct supervision of the Minister of Finance. The measures which are directed towards the improvement of quality and productivity can be grouped under the following headings:

- **Selection of staff and improvement of their performance**
  - tTraining programmes for higher managerial staff on subjects of staff management and management information systems.
  - tTraining programmes for upgrading and updating the knowledge and skills of public officers in their field of work and in the management of software programmes.
  - tImprovement of procedures for recruitment and selection of staff.
  - tImprovement of the system of staff appraisal.
  - tIntroduction of incentives for public officers.
  - tIntroduction of service and performance standards especially in services where output can be measurable.
  - tReview of the system of flexible working hours.

- **Organisation and Functioning of Services**
  - The establishment of a Planning Co-ordination Unit in each ministry under the chairmanship of the Permanent Secretary, consisting of all the Departmental Heads of the Ministry, one officer from the Planning Bureau and one officer from the Public Administration and Personnel Service (PAPS).
  - Examination of the possibility of extending the principle of inter-changeability to the posts of Directors and other senior managerial posts of departments.
  - Simplification of procedures and forms used by the various services with a view to reducing the time required for processing the issues involved.

- Computerisation of the systems used by ministries and departments.

♦ **Working environment**
- Improvement of the buildings that accommodate government employees and improvement of general working conditions.
- Speeding up of the programme of computerisation of the activities of ministries and departments and upgrading of service equipment with emphasis on hardware and software.

♦ **Size and cost of human resources**
- Study of the activities of some public services with a view to amalgamation or abolition of services where necessary and justifiable.
- Strict control on the creation of new posts.
- Freezing of the filling of all first entry posts. Exceptions are only allowed in special cases with the approval of the Minister of Finance.
- Examination towards the abolition of a number of vacant posts with a view to downsizing the government service. Consideration should be given to the fact that the chances of advancement of the existing staff should not be adversely affected.
- Strict control on the recruitment of casual staff and study of the introduction of the method of recruiting on a part-time basis and of contracting out.
- Reduction of overtime work.
- Proposals for the execution of new projects by the various departments should be accompanied by a detailed study of the cost involved in human and other resources.

♦ **Harmonisation with the European Union:** Cyprus has been a candidate member of the European Union (EU) since 1990. However, before joining the EU, the country has to satisfy the following criteria of the Maastricht Agreement:
- fiscal deficit lower than three per cent of the GDP;
- public debt lower than 60 per cent of the GDP;
- inflation lower than 2.5 per cent;
- interest rate lower than seven per cent.

As at 2000, the respective rates of Cyprus' economy were 5.7 per cent instead of 3 per cent in (a), 61 per cent instead of 60 per cent in (b), 4.5 per cent instead of 2.5 per cent in (c) and 7.4 per cent instead of 7 per cent in (d). However, the target is to satisfy the above criteria by 2003, the year in which Cyprus will join the EU. Thus, the implementation of the reform programme of the public sector – reducing the size of the public service, increasing productivity and improving the quality of services offered by the public sector – contributes to the decrease of the fiscal deficit to the required rate.

MALTA

Country Profile

Location: The country comprises an archipelago of six islands and islets in the middle of the Mediterranean Sea, 93km south of Sicily (Italy) and 290km from the coast of North Africa. Malta, Gozo and Comino are inhabitated. The other islands are Cominotto, Filfla and St Paul's Island.

Capital: Valletta

Area: 316 sq km including Comino (3 sq km) and Gozo (67 sq km)

Population: Malta has a population of nearly 400,000. There are no significant ethnic minorities.

Language: The official languages are Maltese and English.

Government: Under the 1964 constitution (amended in 1974 and 1987), Malta is a non-aligned democratic republic with a unicameral House of Representatives. The country has proportional representation using the single transferable vote system. A Party which obtains a majority of votes but minority of seats is allocated additional seats to give it an overall majority of one.

Economy: Malta produces only about 20 per cent of its food needs, has limited freshwater supplies, and has no domestic energy sources. The economy is dependent on foreign trade, manufacturing (especially electronics and textiles), and tourism.

Quality and Productivity Concerns in the Public Sector

In 2000, the public sector had around 31,000 employees within the central government which consists of 90 departments, representing approximately 20 per cent of the working population. Below are major quality and productivity concerns within the sector.

- **Technological Changes:** The fast technological changes that are constantly taking place have affected both the private sector and the public sector alike. New systems of communication and information distribution require new skills and knowledge. Employees within the public service who are most likely to be concerned with technological change need to be prepared through proper training and development.

- **The European Union (EU) Dimension:** The EU poses enormous challenges for officials in the Public Service of Malta. The legislation of the EU and policies affect all the functions of public administration: social services and their provision, social policy, industrial relations, the environment, human resource management, accountability, citizenship, public procurement and the relationship between the state and other local bodies. Therefore, the EU imposes considerable influence on the management of the public service.

- **Local Government:** The introduction of local government in Malta in 1993 (through the establishment of Local Councils) signified new and challenging prospects for the public service. This allowed the central government to concentrate on core public areas, but at the same time it has created tensions between the two levels of government. In view of this, it is felt that public officials need to be adequately trained on the functions of the two levels of government.

- **Decentralisation:** In line with government's policy on decentralisation, departments are now assuming further responsibilities. This gives departments greater autonomy in terms of decision making as long as they satisfy minimum standards or guidelines, which are determined centrally. Decentralisation can, however, be implemented with success so long as continuous monitoring is carried out and if the necessary resources are in place to meet the challenges of new responsibilities in training, human resources and financial management.

Public Sector Reform Issues

The agenda for change in the public sector reflects the three perspectives which have been identified as being the main features of the twenty first century: firstly, the public sector's interaction with society; secondly, the information technology agenda; and thirdly, measures that have been grouped under the general heading of capacity building in the public sector required for healthy growth in the challenging atmosphere that the globalisation process has brought with it.

Improvements in service delivery to the public has been established as the focal point for change in the public service and the following measures have been identified: service delivery improvements in government departments including:
- drawing up Charters in all departments. These will commit departments to delivering services to stated standards (a total of 17 departments have already received their Charters);
- providing one-stop-shop services;
- introducing complaint handling mechanisms; and
- minimising costs for businesses that are a direct product of outmoded bureaucracy.

- An electronic Government Online framework is to provide public services directly to homes and offices. These services range from electronic trading and commerce to the filling and lodging of income tax returns. Electronic terminals are being installed in Local Councils to ensure that 'Government Online' is accessible to everyone. The possibility of accessing services via data transmission through television is also being assessed.

♦ A Central Information Management Unit sets standards for shared information, establishes interdepartmental partnerships for information systems and technology and sets best practices across the public service.

♦ Emphasis is also being placed on the need to continue to improve the institutional framework of the public service in order to support the drive for improved service delivery. Of primary consideration are:
  • the need to promote public-private partnerships;
  • the continued democratisation process leading to further devolution of central functions to local government;
  • the decentralisation of authority in order to empower public officers to effectively manage their organisations;
  • the need to reform the Public Service Commission to enable it assume the role of an appellate body;
  • the introduction of a Public Service Act that defines the values, roles, responsibilities and governing structures of the public service as an institution.

Ownership of the change programme rests with the Public Service Change Co-ordinating Committee chaired by the Permanent Secretary in the Office of the Prime Minister.

PACIFIC

FIJI ISLANDS

Country Profile

Location: The Republic of Fiji Islands lies 1,850km north of Auckland, New Zealand, and 2,800km north east of Sydney, Australia. It consists of about 300 islands (100 inhabited) and 540 islets, spread over 3m sq km. It is surrounded by the island groups of Tuvalu, Wallis and Futuna, Tonga, New Caledonia, Vanuatu and Solomon Islands. The largest islands are Viti Levu ('Great Fiji'), Vanua Levu, Taveuni and Kanduvu.

Capital: Suva

Area: Total land area 18,333 sq km: Viti Levu 10,429 sq km; Vanua Levu 5,556 sq km.

Population: 809,000 (1997) comprising Fijian 51 per cent (predominantly Melanesian with a Polynesian admixture), Indian 44 per cent, European, other Pacific Islanders, overseas Chinese, and other 5 per cent (1998 estimates).

Language: The official language is English.

Government: Fiji Islands became independent on 10 October 1970. The country was declared a republic in 1987. In 1997, the constitution was amended to allow non-ethnic Fijians greater say in government and to make multiparty government mandatory. This entered into force on 28 July 1998. The May 1999 election was the first test of the amended constitution and introduced open voting – not racially prescribed – for the first time at the national level.

Economy: Fiji Islands endowed with forest, mineral, and fish resources, is one of the most developed of the Pacific island economies. The economy is largely agricultural, with the main cash crop and export being sugar cane. Tourism is the largest foreign-exchange earner and clothing exports have grown rapidly in the 1990s. Both sugar and tourism are vulnerable to the climate; hurricanes are relatively frequent and droughts can also cause problems.

Quality and Productivity Concerns in the Public Sector

Major areas of concern in the Fiji Public Service informing the need for reform include:

♦ the high cost of operating government business;

♦ ailing economic environment;

♦ changing technology;

- deteriorating infrastructure, system, procedures and strategies;

- ineffective performance management system, both at organisation and individual levels;

- excessive hierarchical structure.

Public Sector Reform Issues

The following are some of the measures that have been taken to address the areas of concern highlighted above:

- **High cost:** To curb the high level of government expenditure, a zero growth staffing policy was put in place in 1995 that helped in sustaining the size of the overall establishment of government.

- **Corporate Planning:** The corporate plan drive into ministries and departments was initiated by the Public Service Commission through the Management Improvement Division. The major challenge given to the Ministries and Department was to review their processes, systems, procedures and strategies so that they could move away from an input to output base. It was initially difficult for ministries and departments to move away from the traditional way of doing things and they did not see the need to have a corporate plan. However, with consistent promotion and training, ministries and departments now have three-year corporate plans. This effort has brought about significant changes as ministries and departments now know their core outputs for their target clientele. It has also played a major role, particularly for databases for public interface departments such as Immigration, Registrar-General, Road Transport and Public Billing services.

  The other impact of corporate planning has been the undertaking of institutional strengthening exercise in various departments. There has been a shift in direction towards formulating sectoral objectives, strategies, policies and investment programmes/projects. Overall, the corporate plan effort has helped to ensure that sectoral policies and projects are consistent with the national policy and direction.

- **Management Planning:** Ministries and departments are now actively involved in the next phase of the corporate plan, that is, the focusing on the business of the department on an annual basis through management/business plans.

KIRIBATI

Country Profile

Location: Kiribati (pronounced 'Kirabas') is a group of 33 atoll islands located in three major groupings lying along the equator in the Pacific Ocean. They are the Gilbert Islands consisting of 16 inhabited atoll islands including South Tarawa, the seat of government (the Gilbert Islands lies very close to where the international dateline crosses the equator); the Line Islands in the east which has three inhabited islands; and the Phoenix group which lies halfway between the Gilbert and the Lines Islands. Only Kanton in the Phoenix Islands is inhabited.

Capital: Tarawa

Area: Total land area is 717 sq km. The north/south extent is 2,050km.

Population: The population of Kiribati is 81,000 (1997), a third of which reside in South Tarawa, the seat of government.

Language: I-Kiribati and English are spoken. English is the official language, but not much used outside the capital.

Government: The Gilbert Islands were granted self-rule by the United Kingdom in 1971 and complete independence in 1979 under the new name of Kiribati. The United States relinquished all claims to the sparsely inhabited Phoenix and Line Island groups in a 1979 treaty of friendship with Kiribati. Kiribati is a democratic republic with a unicameral legislature.

Economy: Kiribati has few national resources. Commercially viable phosphate deposits were exhausted at the time of independence in 1979. Copra and fish now represent the bulk of production and exports. The economy has fluctuated widely in recent years. Economic development is constrained by a shortage of skilled workers, weak infrastructure and remoteness from international markets.

Quality and Productivity Concerns in the Public Sector

The Kiribati Public Service (KPS) is relatively small and has retained many administrative features of its colonial era. In particular, the colonial response to a small population, widely scattered islands and the lack of commercial potential was to use government resources to provide not only social services, but also basic infrastructure including transport and communication. The cost and inconvenience of decentralisation (a failed attempt carried out after the Second World War) led to a preference for a centralised administration on South Tarawa. To these basic features must be added the realities that colonial policies were often dictated and driven by High Commissioners residing in Fiji, then the Solomon Islands, and that colonial administration was strongly hierarchical and status conscious. These features, which discouraged policy initiatives from below, have left a powerful heritage in the form of a public service which explores and administers policy initiatives from above (ministers) and outside (aid donors) rather than developing alternatives from within. It operates hierarchically among departments, divisions and sections rather than laterally.

As the government is by far the largest employer within Kiribati, the public service is perceived as a source of safe employment, wealth distribution and welfare provision. Indeed, over the past decade, the size of the public service has increased at more than twice the rate of the population. There is, therefore, often a lack of incentive to perform, given the security of government service, as well as inappropriate management reward systems. There is also a lack of pressure to provide cost effective services in a largely non-competitive environment. In some cases, organisations are given multiple objectives with resulting confusion as to whether its aim is to fulfil a social role or to make profit.

Public Sector Reform Issues

Against the background of the foregoing, Kiribati has embarked on a number of reform activities. The following are the main highlights:

- **Retirement age:** The amendment of government policy on the retirement age is one of the major changes that has affected employees of the Kiribati Public Service (KPS). The former retirement age of 50 years was changed and extended to 55 years. The screening and selection of employees to continue working until age 55 is done by the Retirement Committee and approved by the Public Service Commission. This process is strict and only those who have performed exceptionally well and with satisfactory report from their respective employers can continue to work in the KPS. This policy change is also viewed as a reward to those who have continued to maintain their good performance and possess good qualification and experience. Employees who have poor work records are made to leave the service once they reach 50 years of age.

- **'Output basis' budget:** Government has accepted a change to the budget system initiated by the Treasury Department. Because the new budget system is prepared on an 'output basis', government ministries can allocate funds to areas that are considered priority and their performance for each year is easy to measure.

- **Review of the National Conditions of Service (NCS):** The Public Service Office, the core government agency with responsibility for looking after the public service, has embarked on a review of the NCS in line with the national goals and objectives stipulated in the National Development Strategy 1999-2001. In the National Development Strategy, emphasis is put on public sector reform particularly to reduce the size of the public service. Partial privatisation through corporatisation or commercialisation will in effect reduce the size of the public service. Structural unemployment could occur as a result. Accordingly, the Public Service Office through the Technical Assistance provided by the Asian Development Bank will be conducting a research on the impact(s) of structural adjustment emanating, as a result of the reform.

Among other major changes highlighted in the review are the reward management systems, various allowances that different groups of employees are entitled to receive during the course of performing their official duties, appointments, promotions, disciplinary procedures, etc. The present review of the NCS is part of government's attempt to improve working conditions in order to boost the morale of employees and thereby increase their productivity. The review of the NCS is also aimed at streamlining the internal administrative processes with an emphasis on improving timeliness and reducing operational costs.

- **National job evaluation exercise:** This system was introduced to correct anomalies existing within the current grading system of all jobs in the public service. It aims at maintaining an equitable and compatible grading system to ensure satisfaction of all employees.

- **Human Resource Development:** Through the assistance of AusAid and EU aid, it has been possible for the Public Service Office to co-ordinate in-country training programmes in five major sectors of government, namely Fisheries, Agriculture, Public Health, Education and Public Service. The Tarawa Technical Institute (TTI) offers a large number of courses in a range of vocational and technical disciplines, including building and carpentry, computer studies, business studies, adult general education subjects and engineering. The strengthening of the TTI is one of the initiatives taken to increase the institute's capacity to run appropriate courses for government and the private sector. This initiative has also expanded the reach of the TTI through the establishment of learning centres on outer islands. This is a complementary effort to encourage distant learning from the outer islands.

NIUE

Country Profile

Location: Niue is the biggest coral atoll standing on its own in the Pacific Ocean, lying 480km east of Tonga and 930km west of Cook Islands.

Capital: Alofi

Area: 259 sq km

Population: Niue has a population of 1,928 (provisional count October 1999).

Language: The official languages are Niuean and English.

Government: Niue is a self-governing parliamentary democracy. The Niue Constitution Act of 1974 provided for Niue to become self-governing in free association with New Zealand. Under the provision of the Act, close ties are maintained with New Zealand which undertakes responsibility of Niue external relations and defence as well as for the provision of administrative and economic assistance. The Niuean people retain New Zealand citizenship by virtue of this 'special relationship'.

Economy: There is a wide gap between domestic production and demand for goods and service, resulting in Niue's economy being heavily dependent on aid and remittances from New Zealand. Government expenditures regularly exceed revenues, and the shortfall is made up by grants from New Zealand which are used to pay wages to public employees. The agricultural sector consists mainly of subsistence gardening, although some cash crops are grown for export. Industry consists primarily of small factories to process passion fruit, lime oil, honey, and coconut cream. The sale of postage stamps to foreign collectors is an important source of revenue. The island in recent years has suffered a serious loss of population because of migration of Niueans to New Zealand. Efforts to increase GDP include the promotion of tourism and a financial services industry.

Public Sector Reform Issues

Qualified staff are leaving the country for better paid jobs elsewhere, for example New Zealand, Australia and within the pacific region. Prior to 1990, there were about 600 government employees in the public service. At the end of 1990, the total number dropped to 543 due to compulsory redundancy of some staff, notably in the Government Central Stores, Airline and Shipping services as foreign aid dropped. Between 1990 and 1994, there was a further reduction of numbers in the public service to 331. This was achieved via a voluntary redundancy package followed by a policy stating that there would be no further redundancy pay out. The period 1999/2000 has seen the public service figure at about 390 comprising 216 permanent staff while the rest are contract and casual workers, employed only when required for short term projects. The issue now confronting the service is that of surplus to requirement arising from the computerisation of some activities, and also in consideration of the 1994 policy of no further redundancy pay out. The Niue Public Service regulation provides for three months notice and then termination.

Under article 68(1) of the constitution, the Niue Public Service Commission is responsible for reviewing the efficiency and economy of all departments and offices of the executive government. These reviews have the following terms of reference (TOR):

♦ to examine the efficiency and effectiveness of the service given;

♦ critically examine the effectiveness of the current personnel structure relating to the capabilities in providing the services required; and

♦ identify potential areas which are economically viable to be carried out by the private sector.

During the reviews, every employee is asked questions covering all areas of the TOR in both the Niuean and English languages, their responses are collated and recommendations are subsequently presented to the Cabinet for approval. These reviews have over the years have led to the review of the 1979 Niue Public Service Regulations, the update of the Public Service Manual where required, as well as the update of the pay scale, assessment reports and contract agreements.

SAMOA

Country Profile

Location: Samoa is an archipelago of nine islands (five are uninhabited) at the centre of the south west Pacific island groups and is surrounded by Tokelau, American Samoa, tonga, and Waliis and Futuna.

Capital: Apia

Area: 2,831 sq km

Population: Samoa has a population of 168,000 (1997).

Language: Samoan is the official language. English is used in administration and commerce and is widely spoken.

Government: Samoa achieved independence on 1 January 1962, the first South Pacific island country to do so. Since 1962, it has had a Treaty of Friendship with New Zealand. The country is a democracy with a unicameral parliament.

Economy: The economy of Samoa has traditionally been dependent on development aid, private family remittances from overseas and agricultural exports. The country is vulnerable to devastating storms. Agriculture employs two-thirds of the work force, and accounts for 90 per cent of exports which include coconut cream, coconut oil, and copra. Tourism is an expanding sector.

Public Sector Reform Issues

Under the 1992 Human Resource Development plan, the shortage of qualified staff across all government departments became of major concern. The key line staff positions in most disciplines were either vacant for significant periods, or were filled by unqualified staff. Expatriates were, therefore, recruited to meet these needs.

The brain drain in the public service where the young (usually in their twenties and early thirties) and qualified, choose to leave the service for better job opportunities both locally and overseas has been another area of concern. The public service has also been characterised by high inter-departmental staff movement to areas with higher remuneration packages, thus limiting career development in those areas with lower remuneration packages.

One-to-one relationships were common in most departmental management structures and while this was good for the head of department and his/her assistant, other staff members were often not clear about their responsibilities. There was, therefore, an overlap of duties. Coupled with this was the lack of delegation of authority which resulted in poor performance.

The Samoan Public Service underwent its first major transformation since independence in May 1992, when the Cabinet adopted the first Human Resource Plan proposed by the Public Service Commission and assisted by the government of New Zealand. The 1992 Plan formed the basis of subsequent changes which the Commission began implementing in 1993, primarily focussing on personnel categorisation and proper placements in relation to the skills and qualifications of employees. The Commission also began to put together a comprehensive database.

The following changes have been introduced to cater for the shortage of qualified personnel and increasing brain drain in the public service:

◆ professional and specialist staff have been taken out of management positions and treated as internal consultants on renewable contractual basis with remuneration packages that reflect their status;

- in-country training has been given first priority to be followed by regional training;

- upgrading the role and capacity of the Public Service Commission in facilitating and managing the Human Resource Development in a more pro-active manner;

- expatriate personnel are required to incorporate HRD as the primary component in the roles they play while employed in Samoa; and

- an introduction of a comprehensive career planning programme for students at the junior secondary, college and university preparatory year levels.

For organisation structures, the principal strategies identified and implemented are the:

- removal of all one-to-one relationships;

- widening of positions where the criteria for ranking positions are qualifications, length of service and performance;

- reduction of the overlap of functional responsibilities by combining activities into one division or department to allow for effective and efficient utilisation of personnel; and

- job descriptions for all posts, big and small, to ensure that no two persons have the same roles to play simultaneously

In 1995, the Public Service Commission continued with the restructuring process by conducting a Job Analysis and Structural Review Exercise which targeted the most critical positions across the public service, and equating salaries to core work responsibilities and performance.

Public sector reform has also included the introduction of the performance budgeting system and planning for devolution and decentralisation. Standards of service are being improved through good governance, transparency and consistency while the public-private sector partnership is being strengthened. The public sector reform process is expected to lead to a redefinition of the responsibilities of the public service with greater focus on core activities supported by a new customer/client orientation.

The current vehicle for Samoa's public sector reform process is through the Public Service Commission-Institutional Strengthening Project (PSC-ISP), co-funded by AusAID and the Samoa government. The project is managed and controlled by a Steering Committee which has laid down the management framework foundation whereby many current functions of the PSC, including all those of a strictly operational nature, will be devolved to Heads of Departments who will then be accountable for their actions. The framework also indicates that the PSC will be the central human resource agency responsible for setting sector-wide principles and policies, providing advice to the Cabinet and assistance to Heads of Departments in the implementation of those principles and policies, and also monitoring and evaluation departmental performance.

TOKELAU

Country Profile

Location: Tokelau consists of three atoll groups, Atafu, Nukunonu, and Fakaofo, located in the South Pacific 480km north of Apia, Samoa. The atolls are scattered: Atafu lies 64km north west of Nukunonu and Fakaofo 92km south east of Nukunonu.

Capital: Tokelau has no capital.

Area: Atafu (2.03 sq km), Nukunonu (5.46 sq km) and Fakaofo (2.63 sq km) – totalling 10.12 sq km.

Population: About 1600 Tokelau people live on the atolls with at least 5000 residing in New Zealand. Only one main motu (islet) of each atoll is inhabited, except on Fakaofo where a school, hospital, and a few houses are located on another islet

Language: Tokelauan is the official language. English is widely spoken.

Government: In 1948, Tokelau was included 'within the territorial boundaries' of New Zealand, and is thus, a an external territory administered by New Zealand. With the atolls being isolated, each village has developed and operated its own independent social system to meet its traditional needs. The independent existence of each atoll means that there has been no adaptable traditional Tokelau-wide structures to support the trappings of a western type government. Constitutional and administrative arrangements since 1992, based loosely on the Westminster system, has provided Tokelau with delegated powers to enable it to continue developing its own national government.

Economy: Tokelau has many factors which inhibit contemporary development. The 'smallness' factor places limitations on infrastructural economic development, restricts private sector development, and international trade. 'Isolation', on the other hand, exacerbates the effects of small scale. Costs are reflected in the transport and communication sectors because of distances from markets. Finally, it has limited exploitable resources. The net financial asset position of the Tokelau Government is estimated to be negative. The constitutional relationship with New Zealand, however, provides a safety net in terms of Tokelau's modern needs. Recurrent budgetary support from New Zealand through the 1990s accounts for about 80 per cent of total revenue. Expenditures are dominated by grants to villages and departmental costs and about 60 per cent of the national budget is spent on wages and salaries.

Quality and Productivity Concerns in the Public Sector

The Tokelau Public Service (TPS) initially operated from Samoa but was relocated to Tokelau in 1994. Two departments, the Office of the Council of Faipule (OCOF, similar to a Department of Prime Minister and Cabinet) and the Department of Finance and Support Services, are located on each atoll, with the Head Office of the Finance department based in Apia, Samoa. The TPS is legally administered by the New Zealand State Services Commission but there are moves to transfer this responsibility to Tokelau. The total staffing of the public service is about 150 including temporary employees. The existence of the TPS, however, has never been fully acceptable to Tokelau. There are tensions between the traditional authority that each village has had over its labour force and an external or centrally controlled public service.

The significant quality and productivity issues relate to dispersion of staff, isolation and smallness factors. The dispersion of the TPS among the three atolls, in order to support the three executive, who live separately on each atoll, raises the costs of inter-atoll co-ordination or rationalisation of some activities. The causes include the need to triplicate some of the services (for example, hospital care, schooling to a certain level and electricity generation). Moreover, the isolation factor adds to costs because of the limitations of transportation services and telecommunications system. Limitations in these two services adversely affect the quality of information and overall efficiency of the system.

The smallness factor means having a limited number of local personnel with the required skills and experience to manage self-government on each atoll group and particularly to support the Executive undertake its role. This has been addressed partially by contracting Tokelauans from overseas.

Public Sector Reform Issues

Broadly, the objective of the public sector reforms is to redistribute departmental functions, between central government and the three villages according to the following principles: service delivery functions should generally be transferred to the three villages; and policy, regulatory, and funding functions and other selected services should remain in the TPS. (Selected services refer to any functions which it is appropriate for the centre to deliver, for instance, a central registry of births, marriages and deaths would be retained in the centre because it is crucial to legal and constitutional issues regarding citizenship.) The goal, apart from divesting functions to the villages, is to establish a more enduring relationship between the nation and each village.

The following initiatives have enhanced the provision of advice and services of the TPS:

- **Relocation of TPS from Samoa to Tokelau:** There is better interaction between the leadership and officials; officials are more responsive to clients; quality information regarding local conditions and impact of programmes are better captured in policy advice and delivery.

- **Improved telecommunication system:** There is inter-atoll linkage and with the outside world via a satellite telephone system.

- **Information technology:** The use of computers and e-mail facility have been introduced. The practice of drafting Cabinet papers through e-mail is becoming routine though subject to the vagaries of the satellite system.

- **Interactive satellite education programme:** Linking Tokelau to the South Pacific University through an interactive satellite education programme will introduce on site training and further learning opportunities for the people and the TPS.

REFERENCES

Adamolekun, L (ed) (1999), *Public Administration in Africa: Main Issues and Selected Country Studies*, Boulder, Colorado, Westview Press

Adedeji, A. (1995) 'Transferring Successful Transition Experiences' (Africa), in *Government in Transition*. London: Commonwealth Secretariat.

Agere, S (2000), *Promoting Good Governance: Principles, Practices and Perspectives*, London: Commonwealth Secretariat

Ayeni, V (ed.) (1992), *Civil Service Transformation for Structural Adjustment*, Lagos: NIM & University of Lagos Press

Ayeni, V (ed) (1997), 'Public Administration in Africa', *Special Issue of Politeia* (Pretoria), 16, 2

Ayeni, V (2001), *Empowering the Customer: The Citizen in Public Sector Reform*, London: Commonwealth Secretariat

Baker, R (ed) (1992), *Public Administration in Small and Island States*, West Hartford, Connecticut: Kumarian Press

Barenstein, J. (1994), *Overcoming Fuzzy Government in Bangladesh*. Dhaka: University Press Limited

Bertram, G. and Walters, R.F. ((1985), The MIRAB Economies in the South Pacific Microstate, *Pacific Viewpoint*, 26(3).

CIA. (2001), The World Factbook 2001. Washington DC: Central Intelligence Agency

Civil Liberties Organisation: (1991), *Annual Report on Human Rights 1990*. Lagos: Jeromdaiho and Associates.

Corkey, J et al (eds) (1998), *Management of Public Service Reform: A Comparative Review of Experiences in the Management of Programmes of the Administrative Arm of Central Government*, Brussels: Amsterdam: IOS Press & Brussels, IIAS

Commonwealth Secretariat. (1995), A *Profile of the Public Service of Malaysia*. London: Commonwealth Secretariat.

Commonwealth Secretariat. (1995), A *Profile of the Public Service of Malta*. London: Commonwealth Secretariat.

Commonwealth Secretariat. (1995), A *Profile of the Public Service of Trinidad and Tobago*. London: Commonwealth Secretariat.

Commonwealth Secretariat. (1997), A *Profile of the Public Service of Zimbabwe*. London: Commonwealth Secretariat.

Cyprus: *Strategic Development Plan 1999-2003*.

Davies, A.E. 'Executive – Legislative Relations and Democratization during the Transition Programme', in Gboyega A. *Corruption and Democratization* in Nigeria. Ibadan: Agbo Area Publishers.

Davis, C. (1999), Lectures: *Public Sector Reform in Jamaica, The Executive Agency Concept; Reforming the Cabinet Office, Strengthening the Core of Government*. Kingston: Jamaica Civil Service.

Singapore. (2000), 'e-Government: The Next Digital Wave', *Experience Singapore*.

Finnemore, M. and Van Rensburg, R. (1999), *Contemporary Labour Relations*. Durban: Butterworths.

Giber, D. et al (2000), *Best Practices in OD and HRD Handbook*. *Lexington*, MA: Linkage Inc.

Government of Belize. (2000), *Public Sector Reform: Charting the Way Forward – 2000 and Beyond*. Government Printer.

Government of St Lucia. *Green Paper on Public Sector Reform*. Castries: Office of Public Sector Reform.

Government of St Lucia. (2000), *White Paper on Public Sector Reform*. Office of Public Sector Reform.

Government of Uganda. (1998), *Education Strategic Investment Plan 1998-2003*.

Green, R. (ed.) (2000), *The Commonwealth Yearbook 2000*. Norwich: The Stationery Office.

Hayes, R.H. and Pisano, G.P. (1994) 'Beyond World-Class: The New Manufacturing Strategy', *Harvard Business Review*, January/February, 7786.

Jalan, B. (ed.) (1982), *Problems and Policies in Small Economies*. London: Croom Helm.

Kaul, M. (1995), *From Problem to Solution: Commonwealth Strategies for Reform*, London: Commonwealth Secretariat

Kiribati. *National Development Strategy 1999-2001*.

Malaysia. (2000), *The Public Service of Malaysia*. Putrajaya: Malaysian Administration Modernization and Management Planning Unit.

Mauritius. (2000), *The Reform of the Civil Service: Report of a Standing Committee*. Government Printing Press.

Nigeria. (1997), *Report of the Vision 2010 Committee, Main Report*. Vision 2010 Secretariat.

OECD. (1998), *Putting Citizens First, Portuguese Experience in Public Management Reform*. Public Management Occasional Papers No. 13.

Peretz, D, et. al. (eds) (2001), *Small States in the Global Economy*, London: Commonwealth Secretariat & The World Bank

Politt, C and Bouchaert, G (2000), *Public Management Reform: A Comparative Perspective*, Oxford: Oxford University Press

Rugumamu, S.M. (ed.) (1998), *Civil Service Reform in Tanzania: Proceedings of the National Symposium, January 15-16, 1998*.

Rugumyamheto, J.A. and Munishi, G.K. (1998), *Eastern and Southern Africa Consultative Workshop on Civil*

Service Reforms, Workshop Report. Arusha March 4-6, 1998.

Scott, I and Thynne, I (eds) (1994), *Public Sector Reform: Critical Issues and Perspectives*, Hong kong, AJPA

Selwyn, P. (1975), *Development in Small Countries*. London: Croom Helm.

South Africa. (1997), *Basic Conditions of Employment Act*, No. 75 of 1997.

South Africa. (1998), *Employment Equity Act*, Act No. 55 of 1998

South Africa. (1995), *Labour Relations Act*, No. 66 of 1995

South Africa. (1999), *Public Service Amendment Act*, Act No. 5 of 1999

South Africa. (1997), *Public Service Commission Act*, Act No. 46 of 1997

South Africa. (April 1999), *Public Service Management Development Programme*. Mid-term Review.

South Africa. (1997), *White Paper on Public Service Education and Training*. Pretoria: Government Printers.

South Africa. (1995), *White Paper on the Transformation of the Public Service*. Pretoria: Government Printers.

Tanzania. (1996), *Civil Service Reform Programme: Vision Strategy and Action Plan 1996 – 1999*. Dar es Salaam: Civil Service Department.

Tanzania. (1999), *Code of Ethics and Conduct for the Public Service*, *Tanzania*.

Tanzania. (1999), *Public Service Reform Programme: Strategy and Action Plan (2000 – 2004)*.

Tanzania. (1999), *Public Service Management and Employment Policy*.

The Gambia. (1999), *National Governance Programme Document*.

Tokelau. (1999), *Green Paper for Discussion with Tokelau Regarding Transfer of Employment Responsibility and Related Issues*. State Services Commission.

Turner, M and Hulme, D (1997), *Governance, Administration and Development: Making the State Work*, West Hartford, Connecticut, Kumarian Press

Trinidad and Tobago. (1994), *Regional Health Authority Act*.

Trinidad and Tobago. (1997), *Towards a New Public Administration*. Port of Spain: Ministry of Public Administration and Information.

UNDP. (1993), *Report on Public Administration Sector Study in Bangladesh*. Dhaka: UNDP.

Uganda. (1996), *Uganda Civil Service Reform Programme: Status Report 8, 1 January – 31 March 1996*. Kampala: Ministry of Public Service.

Uganda. (1998), *Education Strategic Investment Plan (ESIP) 1998-2003 Work Plan*. Kampala: Education Planning Department, Ministry of Education and Sports.

Uganda. (1992), 'Government White Paper on the *Education Policy Review Commission Report*'.

Uganda. (1997), Local Government Act.

Uganda. (1999), 'Report of the Inter-Ministerial Task Force on Improving Payroll Management'.

Vandersyp, C.J. et al (1998), *Review of the Framework to NZODA to Tokelau, April 1998.*

Vicere, A.A. and Fulmer, R.M. (1997), *Leadership by Design.* Boston MA: Havard Business School Press.

LIST OF CONTRIBUTORS

Name	Country
Ablo, Mawutor	Ghana
Afif, Mohammed	Seychelles
Agarwal, Shekhar	India
Alailima, Patricia J	Sri Lanka
Ali, Daud	Fiji Islands
Apedo, Gasute Theodore	Ghana
Attipoe, Alice E	Ghana
Belaman, Idris	Brunei Darussalam
Belford-Sua, Laititi	Samoa
Bodie, Donella	The Bahamas
Bundhun, Nizamuddin	Mauritius
Callwood, Josephine	British Virgin Islands
Campbell, Marsha Nicole	The Bahamas
Chichava, A	Mozambique
Choudhury, Faisal Ahmed	Bangladesh
Christian, Colmore S	Dominica
Cole, Adul Rahman	The Gambia
Confait, Charles	Seychelles
Dassanayake, Leela	Sri Lanka
Dayanandan, Swapna	Singapore
Dias, Errol	Seychelles
Didi, Ahmed Hassan	Maldives
Evehe, Jeannine Angele Sidonie	Cameroon
Fathee, Moosa	Maldives
Hasbollah, Hajah Rosliah	Brunei Darussalam
Hlope, Nomathemba	Swaziland
Hurng, Sio Wei	Singapore
Jayaweera	Sri Lanka
Jeewah, A S	Mauritius
Kasali, T K	Nigeria
Kitchoff, Ruan	South Africa
Kotadadeniya, H M S	Sri Lanka
Lamin, J P K	Sierra Leone
Lee, Ark Boon	Singapore
Lee, Florence	Montserrat
Lyners, John	South Africa

Makambwe, G F	Zambia
Madula, S T K	Malawi
Mitala, John	Uganda
Mitchell, Minette D	Jamaica
Mohammed, Vade R	Trinidad and Tobago
Mokgoro, T J	South Africa
Morgan, J Paul	Jamaica
Nagu, Mary M	Tanzania
Nannono, Mary Lubowa	Uganda
Ndifon, Lenga Philip	Cameroon
Noordin Hajah Hindun	Brunei Darussalam
Oagile, M	Botswana
Okafor, Augustine O	Nigeria
Parellis M	Cyprus
Pasisi, U	Niue
Poitier, Eugene	The Bahamas
Ragen, S	Mauritius
Rahiman, H	Malaysia
Rahman, Talebar	Bangladesh
Rahman, Ahmad A	Brunei Darussalam
Rakauti, I	Kiribati
Ramaite, Muthanyi Robinson	South Africa
Roebeck, Tailino	Samoa
Sammut, Simon	Malta
Sandhu, R	India
Sebego, L K	South Africa
Sebopeng, Robby Bahakae	Botswana
Shareef, Huda Ali	Maldives
Silao, Aleki	Tokelau
Soonarane, S M K	Mauritius
Soong, Corrinne	Singapore
Tabane-Masutha, M D	South Africa
Tiboth, David	Namibia
Timeon, Ioataake	Kiribati
Toleafoa, K Samoa Tooki, M	Kiribati
Tooma, Wirki	Kiribati
Welch, Sylvester	Barbados
Yambesi, G D	Tanzania